HARBOUR OFFICE
THE KING CHARLES
PARADISE ST
OLD TOWN HOUSE
NO LEFT TURN
OAKLEY BROS
Poole

**1953-1963**

by

**JOHN HILLIER & MARTIN BLYTH**

Designed by Graham Smith

POOLE HISTORICAL TRUST

1994

This volume is published by the Poole Historical Trust, whose primary aims are the promotion of research, and the publication of works on the history and life of Poole and the surrounding area.



**PREVIOUS PUBLICATIONS**

The Pride of Poole
An Album of Old Poole
Mansions and Merchants of Poole & Dorset
Brownsea Islander
Poole and World War II
Portfolio of Old Poole
Ebb-Tide at Poole
History of the Town of Poole, 1839 (reprint)
Art in Poole & Dorset
Victorian Poole
Poole After World War II
D-Day Poole



First Published October 1994
ISBN 1 873535 15 5



Design and production Andrew Arnold

Book printed and bound in Great Britain by
Biddles Limited, Guildford and King's Lynn

## CONTENTS



Index compiled by Martin Blyth

## ACKNOWLEDGEMENTS

We are grateful to Poole Reference Library and Poole Corporation for assistance in research, and to the Poole Museums Service for copying some of the photographs.

Photographs and illustrations used in the text pages have kindly been supplied by the following:
Alderney Junior School: page 23 (top), Mrs Margaret Allen: page 178.
Annette Bailey: page 36 (top), Mrs Phyllis Bravery: pages 54 (both), 55 (both),
Barbara Bristowe: pages 16 (top), 17 (top), 49,
Ernest Bristowe: pages 18 (bottom), 25, 90, 92 (bottom), 93 (both), 144 (bottom),
David Davis: pages 20, 21, 170, 171 (top), Mrs Clara Douie: pages 108, 109 (bottom), 110,
Noel R Hardwick: page 36 (bottom),
Andrew Hawkes Collection:
pages 24, 43, 45 (both), 50 (bottom), 52 (top), 53, 140 (inset), 141 (both), 149 (top).
E B Latcham: pages 164, 165 (top), Parkstone Grammar School: page 23 (bottom),
Poole & Dorset Herald: pages 8, 10, 140 (bottom).
Poole Corporation: pages 22, 50 (top), 97, 127 (all), 135, 138, 140 (top), 144 (top), 146.
Poole Hospital: pages 56 (bottom), 57.
Poole Museums Service:
pages 26 (top), 28, 42, 46 (bottom), 48, 83, 85, 86 (both), 88 (top), 103, 106, 107, 150.
Poole Official Guide: page 19, Edith Roberts: pages 122, 123, 124 (both), 125 (top).
S A H Swain: page 101, W B Tucker & Son: page 72,
Photographs on pages 7, 13, 14, 16 (bottom), 17 (bottom), 26 (bottom), 27,37, 44, 46 (top), 47, 51, 52 (bottom), 58, 60, 62, 63, 64, 66, 67, 69, 71, 82, 84, 87, 89, 99, 100, 109 (top), 113, 116, 120, 125 (bottom), 131 (both), 132, 133, 134, 137, 148, 149 (bottom), 152, 155 (both), 157, 159, 160, 162, 165 (bottom), 166, 168 (both), 169, 171 (bottom), 176 (both), 177, 182, 183, 184, 185, 187, 188, 189 (both), 190, 191, 192, 193, 196, 199, 201, 202, 203, 204, and 205 are copyright 1994 by Martin Blyth.

It has not been possible to ascertain the source of other illustrations used in the text.

# Preface

The prospect of a new Elizabethan age, when the nation could prosper and enjoy the fruits of victory, was dashed in the nineteen-fifties by economic stringency, made worse by new wars which broke out in the Far East, the Middle East, and Africa.

The Government struggled to attain economic stability by alternate periods of 'stop' as the economy overheated, and 'go' when fearing a slump. Local government expenditure was considered as part of the Government's costs and was severely controlled. Some council projects were rejected, and others were delayed, either by controls or by the shortage of materials.

Yet the spirit of Poole people, and their determination to achieve long overdue improvements to services and amenities, never wavered: and this despite the controversy that some changes were bound to provoke, not to mention the vagaries of outlook and political fortune which could then occur through the system of annual municipal elections.

Of the 39 members of Poole Borough Council, only ten remained on the council throughout the decade covered in this book. This seemed to have little effect upon the consistency with which some fought for change, even though there were always others who feared it; or upon the awareness, on both sides of the debate, of what it could entail for an ancient borough whose character, however behind the times it might be, remained endearing.

Perhaps this was the issue that encouraged them to put their views with such zeal and sincerity: the spirit of Poole, and how to preserve it, even if some of the judgements had to be taken on trust. For this was all a long time ago, when notions of conservation, community and heritage did not always survive the post-war passion for renewal and modernisation as well as they did in Poole.

By the standards of today, it was a decidedly old-fashioned era. The Headmaster of Poole Grammar School complained about the difficulty of enforcing the rule that boys' haircuts should be short back and sides; the principal of the Technical College was unhappy about students smoking and dancing to rock'n'roll music during the lunch break; and the borough Magistrates ordered photographs of the sculptures of Pompeii to be destroyed as obscene. It is unlikely that any of these worthy citizens would have had the slightest qualms about their own notions of propriety, or felt themselves at risk from the sort of easy ridicule that would degenerate into barren cynicism during the next decade.

Unaware of the vast changes in society and its attitudes that lay just over the horizon, the town's leaders set out their vision for the future of Poole, and what they wished to see preserved from its past. It is no task of this volume to appraise the merits of that vision from a distant standpoint; only to explain how it contributed to the town as it is today, and to leave readers better informed to pass, if they wish, the judgements of hindsight.

John Hillier Martin Blyth

*The King Charles Inn, Thames Street, 1962.*

*'Throughout all my life and with all my heart,
I shall strive to be worthy of your trust.'*

*Queen Elizabeth II in her broadcast to the nation on the evening of her coronation.*

*The civic party from Poole outside 10 Downing Street, from left to right - Wilson Kenyon, Town Clerk; Lady Digby; Captain Pilkington; Fred Reeves; Geoffrey Bravery; Charles Wells; Sir Mervyn Wheatley; Lord Digby; Mary Llewellin.*

# The New Elizabethans

Nearing the end of the century, we have come a long way from the start of what so many citizens, in Poole and throughout the nation, felt moved to acclaim as a new era of hope and prosperity. When Queen Elizabeth II was crowned on 2nd June 1953, it brought a sense of public rejoicing that went beyond the pomp and pageantry of the ancient rituals. The time had arrived for the nation to turn its back on the sufferings and privations of the second world war and its immediate aftermath.

Earlier that year, income tax was reduced. Rationing of eggs and sweets had at last been ended. On the eve of Coronation Day it was announced that a British expedition had become the first to conquer the summit of Mount Everest. A day or so later, British sports cars had an overwhelming success in the Le Mans 24-hour race. The nation was in confident mood as its newspapers hailed the dawning of a glorious New Elizabethan age.

Like other towns and cities throughout the land, Poole was invited to send its own civic representatives to witness the proceedings in London. The mayor, Miss Mary Llewellin, was in the Westminster Abbey congregation, and two members of the council were allotted seats in the stands outside. All signs of the war had been removed from the route of the royal procession: and for weeks afterwards, the lavish decorations throughout the heart of London would still be attracting hordes of sightseers from all over the country.

It was less than twelve months since the area served by BBC television had been extended to include Poole. The Coronation prompted many people to buy their first set. Hundreds of others, including pensioners, watched the ceremony on sets specially installed in church halls at Lower Parkstone and Hamworthy. But television was not yet widespread enough to have acquired its controversial power to dominate our perception and celebration of historic events. So the numbers who celebrated around a television screen were dwarfed by those for whom taking an active part in festivities of many kinds was more important than viewing the occasion which gave rise to them.

Poole's official celebrations began with the ringing of church bells throughout the borough. There was a civic parade, followed by a thanksgiving service, in Poole Park, attended by council members, magistrates, and contingent's from the armed forces, ex-Servicemen's associations, the fire and civil defence services and other organisations. The Loyal Address sent by the Corporation to the Queen was read out, and the deputy mayor, Alderman Geoffrey Bravery, took the salute at a march past. When loudspeakers in the park began to relay the BBC radio commentary on the Coronation, it was the signal for the start of a day of special events which took place throughout the borough's parks, on Poole Quay, and in the harbour, ending with a Boy Scouts' torchlight procession and bonfire on Constitution Hill.

Many parents resolved to give their children a day to remember by banding together with their neighbours to organise street parties, which on Coronation Day itself and over the following weekend, were to be one of the most widespread forms of celebration. Houses, gardens and streets were decked with flags and bunting. Tables and chairs were brought out into the centre of the road, and laid with a huge tea, before which there might be sports or a fancy dress parade. Then there would be more games in the street or a nearby playground - or perhaps Maypole dancing and fireworks - before bedtime, when the grown-ups took over and danced on into the night.

Carefully hoarded stores of dried fruit and other ingredients were made into Coronation cakes, some of which weighed more than a quarter of a hundredweight. One street on the Bourne Estate had a cake more than two feet long, decorated to look like The Mall, complete with a gilded State Coach. In another, neighbours baked more than a thousand cakes for a tea party for 180 children. The Coronation Day weather in Poole, alas, did not favour the celebrations. It was inclined to be dull and showery, and many organisers made plans to transfer their parties to halls or marquees in case it rained. Some were determined to have their tea outside, come rain or shine. At one party in Alderney, all the tablecloths were soaked by a sudden downpour. Those in charge simply re-laid the tables and carried on. It might have been the dawning of a new era, but for the British climate, and traditional British stoicism, it was business as usual.

Coronation Year would also have been an ideal time at which to see the fulfilment of the borough council's resolution, carried as long ago as 7th May 1946, that Sir Winston Churchill, who had led the nation to victory as its wartime Prime Minister, should be admitted to the roll of Honorary Freemen. But it was not to be.

Churchill had become Prime Minister again late in 1951, and the townspeople could understand that he would not be able to come to Poole to receive the Honorary Freedom, even though they were disappointed when this news reached them in 1952. The letter to the Town Clerk stated that Churchill would let him know when he would be able to receive the honour during the following year. After making tentative arrangements for a ceremony to take place in London at the Savoy Hotel, the council was disappointed not to be notified of a date in 1953. Its members were unaware that Sir Winston had suffered a serious stroke in June of that year.

Then there was another setback. Churchill wrote to suggest the date of 5th May 1954, but scotched the council's grand plans for a ceremony at the Savoy. Instead, he suggested, a 'small delegation' should attend at 10 Downing Street. The council, for all its disappointment, immediately accepted the invitation and appointed its delegation. Its representatives were to be the Mayor (Miss Mary Llewellin), the Recorder (Malcolm McGougan); Alderman Bravery, the Deputy Mayor; Charles Wells, the Sheriff; Alderman Reeves, the Mayor-elect; Alderman Lloyd-Allen, chairman of the finance committee; and Wilson Kenyon, the Town Clerk. In addition, Lord Digby, HM Lieutenant for Dorset, Richard Pilkington, the Member of Parliament for Poole, and Sir Mervyn Wheatley, his predecessor as Member of Parliament, were invited.

A few weeks earlier the council had bought its first Mayoral car, a second-hand 1930 Lincoln Royal limousine, a model said to have been Ford's answer to the Rolls-Royce, which had previously been on hire to the council for civic duties. Although it was a large six-seater car, it still could not accommodate the entire Poole delegation, so a second car was hired for the occasion. It set out for London behind the Mayoral Lincoln.

On the way, there was nearly a calamitous accident. As the Mayor's car was passing a coal lorry that was stationary on the other side of the road, a car coming the other way started to pull out around the lorry. The Mayor's car was just able to avoid a collision, but the hired car behind had to veer off the road. It landed on its side, throwing the passengers into a heap. Aldermen Lloyd-Allen and Bravery landed on top of Sir Mervyn. They had to escape through the window of the driver's door.

None of the passengers had been seriously hurt, but it now seemed they had no alternative to being squeezed into the Mayor's car for the rest of their journey. They were late arriving for lunch, which had been arranged at Mr McGougan's club in St James's Street, but were able to tidy up before proceeding to Downing Street. Here, they were invited into the drawing room to meet Sir Winston, who had already been joined by members of his family, including Mr and Mrs Sandys and Captain Soames, as well as Lady Digby. Chairs for the ceremony had been arranged in a semi-circle around a high-back settee on which Churchill was seated, dressed in a dark suit with a polka-dot tie.

Miss Llewellin made a short speech, referring to his inspirational leadership of the country during the second world war, to his family connections with Dorset, and to his namesake who had been made a Freeman of Poole in 1660. She then asked the Town Clerk to read the council's resolution admitting Sir Winston to the roll of Honorary Freemen. After he signed the Freeman's Roll,

Miss Llewellin presented him with a silver casket to contain the Certificate of Admission.

Sir Winston, in his reply, said: 'I have had a great many Freedoms presented to me, and have not been able to receive half of them, but I hope to live long enough to accomplish this task.'

He said he had often been to Poole, particularly when he was First Lord of the Admiralty, and could remember, in particular, a review there, with ships gathering in the harbour before sailing to Scapa Flow. 'I have been back many times, sometimes on pleasure and often on business, and have the warmest feelings for your town. I hope - indeed, I earnestly hope - that I shall go back again to see the scene I know so well.'

Thanking the council for its gift, he declared: 'Keeping these traditions plays a great part in strengthening the life and strength of the community, and makes them rise superior to the endless clatter and chatter of day-to-day events which tend to overshadow our life from time to time.'

*'I have been back (to Poole) many times,*
*sometimes on pleasure and often on business,*
*and have the warmest feelings for your town.'*

*Sir Winston Churchill, 1954.*

*Churchill receives the Freedom of Poole from the Mayor, Miss M M Llewellin.*

*The changing face of the Old Town, seen from the shell of the former Black Horse public house.*

*Awaiting new accommodation this boy and his sister, together with their mother and a young baby, spent a night sleeping rough in an alleyway off High Street after the family was evicted from a nearby flat.*

# Getting Up to Date

## Housing

The New Elizabethans of 1953 had declared their loyalty and hopes for better times ahead. In Poole, the borough council faced the task of transforming these aspirations into urgently needed new homes, schools and other public services.

The most urgent problem at the end of the second world war had been the desperate shortage of housing. The Government took complete control of scarce building materials and at first, allowed only local authorities to build new houses. Councils were later allowed to license private builders to provide, subject to price controls, a strictly limited number of houses. As a result, by 1951, Poole Council had built 1,514 houses and flats, against 744 erected by private builders. When these controls on private builders were abolished in 1953, they took full advantage of their new freedom, so that by 1963, they had erected 5,945 homes, compared with 3,944 provided by the council.

A considerable proportion of the council's housing was built by its own Works Department, established in 1946. Though it had to compete for contracts against private builders, it would by 1963 have built over 1,500 new homes, as well as three new schools, and extensions to six other schools. Profits from its activities contributed £35,000 to the reduction of rate demands.

By 1962 the main housing estates of the Corporation had been built. Bourne Estate (456 houses), Trinidad (325), Alderney (388) and Waterloo (750) were complete, and 286 of 836 houses planned for Turlin Moor had been erected. New homes had to be provided for hundreds of families dispossessed by slum clearance and redevelopment in the Old Town, many of whom had long-established connections with that part of Poole. They were assured they would be given the opportunity to move back to that area if they wished; but in the early days of the slum clearance programme, not enough land became available for large scale redevelopment.

The council's policy of building as many new homes as possible in, or near, the Old Town meant that high-density blocks of flats had to be provided. By 1962 the programme was well under way. The Works Department completed Lagland Court (50 flats) in 1960, and a private firm completed another 14 flats in Skinner Street the following year. Two ten-storey blocks, each of 57 flats, and one four-storey block of 20 flats, were built at Sterte in 1960-61. In 1962, Nelson Court (63 flats) was completed in the Old Town, and contracts were signed for the erection of two further 11-storey blocks, Rodney Court and Drake Court, each of 62 flats.

*(Left) Lagland Court flats.*

*(Bottom) One of the 'bomb sites' created by slum clearance in the Old Town.*

(Left) *New blocks of flats were rising while slum clearance proceeded, 1962.*

(Bottom) *Sterte Court, 1962: a new tenant surveys the view from the balcony of her high-rise flat.*

The boom in private housebuilding meant the disappearance of many farms and nurseries which once surrounded the main built-up areas of Poole, as well as a number of old houses that had been among the landmarks of outlying areas. Tatnam, Creekmoor, Harkwood, Milepost and Northbrook Farms were engulfed. Eleven acres of Parkstone Golf Course were sold for residential development. Surging land prices transformed nurseries in Upper Parkstone, Oakdale, and Broadstone into building sites, and affected many existing properties which had extensive grounds. Some of these, such as Wilderton House, Stromboli Crest and Blake Dene House, survived, at the

*(Above) Dorchester School, previously house owned by William Pearce who established the Poole Foundry.*
*(Below) The 'Castle', Castle Hill.*

expense of losing most of their grounds. Others, such as 'The Castle' and its 27 acres of land on Castle Hill, in Parkstone, and Dorchester School, with its eight and a half acres at the foot of the hill, disappeared altogether, as did some homes in The Avenue and Lindsay Road, Branksome Park. It was the value of the land that mattered, regardless of the age of the property or its architectural value. The same considerations affected the town's hotels. The grounds of Canford Cliffs Hotel, most of which was destroyed during the war, were sold off for housing development. The same fate later befell the Branksome Court, another hotel in Canford Cliffs. The owners of other hotels sought planning consent for similar schemes. They included the prestigious Branksome Tower Hotel, where the council's refusal of consent was overturned on appeal. It was saved only by an hotel chain buying it.

*The Branksome Tower Hotel.*

Many private residents in areas such as Branksome Park and Canford Cliffs were not happy at the prospect of extensive flat development. They voiced their objections at a public meeting in December 1959 which was told that in the preceding 18 months, the council had received more than 500 applications for permission to build flats. There was consternation at the way in which an original permission could be later increased in size, and at the heights of some

*The Ferry Café.*

applications. One applicant submitted plans for a 12-storey block, 109 feet high, on the site of the Ferry Café, overlooking the harbour mouth at Sandbanks. At a public inquiry following its rejection, it was claimed that Dorset County Council's Planning Committee, which supported the proposal, considered that such a tower would provide a 'sentinel' or 'terminal feature' and 'punctuate the landscape' at the mouth of Poole Harbour. These suggestions were given their come-uppance in the report of the Government inspector, Mr (later Professor) Colin Buchanan, when permission was refused in 1960. He saw them as rather desperate attempts at justification. 'The landscape requires none of these things,' he wrote, 'all it needs is to be left alone.'

*I walk the asphalt paths of Branksome Chine*
*In resin-scented air like strong Greek wine*
*And dream of cliffs of flats along those heights,*
*Floodlit at night with green electric lights.*

That was John Betjeman in his poem *The Town Clerk's Views,* which used the voice of an imaginary chief executive to savage and satirise a national catalogue of what the poet described as 'plans to turn our country into hell.' Today, for reasons of security, there may be much more floodlighting installed around houses and flats than hitherto: but in the main, the effect of greenery, in Branksome Park and elsewhere, is due to the tree preservation orders made by the council to lessen the impact of a great deal of new building. By 1962,

*The Ferry Café being demolished.*

more than 1,400 acres of the borough had been protected.

Ever more florid language was employed at town planning appeals by would-be flat developers. Canford Cliffs was castigated as an 'upper-income bracket subtopia' and Branksome Park described as 'quite dead.' But by 1963, the boom appeared to have run its course, and the council decided to review the changes to its policy on flat development in Branksome Park, Canford Cliffs and Sandbanks, which had caused so much controversy when they were introduced less than three years earlier. It did so after the Town Planning Committee reported that out of 586 new flats built in the borough, 163 were still unoccupied, and all but twenty-seven of the unoccupied flats were in those selfsame areas.

## Education

Herbert Carter, an alderman of Poole from 1905 to 1948, and a freeman from 1928, was the author of several books in which he reflected upon its past, present and future destiny. He did not exaggerate when he wrote, in *I Call to Mind*, that Poole had started the second world war short of houses and with too few schools. The latter problem was exacerbated after the war, not only by a rapidly rising population, but by the raising of the school leaving age to 15.

Though the Government maintained strict controls on building, some slow, but significant, progress had been made by 1953. Herbert Carter Secondary School, Sylvan Road and Trinidad infants' schools had been built, and many existing ones extended, either by adding temporary buildings or by abandoning nursery classes. The next decade also saw the completion of new primary schools at Alderney and Hillbourne, and new premises for Parkstone Grammar School at Waterloo. Its old premises at Lower Parkstone were converted for use by the new Ashley Cross Secondary School. The grave shortage of accommodation had meant that for seven years, until 1962, junior pupils from Broadstone and Waterloo had to be transported to and from South Road School in the Old Town; while at Henry Harbin Secondary School in 1958, a former air raid shelter was converted for use as a classroom.

*(Above) Hillbourne Primary School, 1956.*

*(Top right) The Headmaster, Mr L T Bennett, and his staff, at the opening of Alderney Junior School.*

*(Bottom right) Miss Winifred Allen, the former Headmistress, accompanied by Ald. A J Stokes, Mayor, lays the foundation for the new Parkstone Grammar School in Sopers Lane, Waterloo.*

This foundation stone
was laid by
Miss W·M·Allen M·A
Headmistress 1937-59
6 · 0

During the same decade, Dorset County Council undertook the building of the first part of the new Poole Technical College premises in North Road, Parkstone. Though most of Poole's education services had been delegated to the borough Education Committee, the County Council retained responsibility for further education. By 1960 the county Education Committee was faced with desperate overcrowding at the college, and recommending the the erection of four huts for use as temporary classrooms. The second stage of the building programme had failed to gain Ministry of Education approval for a start to be made in 1961-62. At the same time, according to the head of the department of commerce and general education at the college, more parents and children were seeing the benefits of remaining in full-time education when the General Certificate of Education was increasingly demanded as a qualification by employers and institutions. By the following year, the number of enrolments into the department would have more than doubled since 1955.

The number of births in Poole in 1962 was 1,581, compared with 1,147 in 1953, and local classrooms were already full. At the end of 1962, 108 out of 213 primary school classes had more than 36 pupils. In the 106 secondary school classes, 76 had more than 31 pupils, and 34 had more than 36 per class. The education committee was having to run hard just to keep abreast of its problems, but there was already hope that they would be alleviated. The same year saw work progressing on the second Heatherlands School and Saint Edward's Roman Catholic Secondary School, while Kemp-Welch Boys' and Girls' Secondary Schools were being extended to take 600 pupils each.

*Poole Grammar School, Kingland Road.*

Ministerial approval had also been obtained for the building of new premises for Poole Grammar School at Gravel Hill, which would start the following year. The former premises in Kingland Road would then accommodate the new Seldown Secondary School.

*'Bread pudding is still the favourite in school meals'*

*Poole Herald 1954.*

## Roads and Transport

Of the many problems created by a sharp increase in traffic during the decade, few in Poole were more acute than those involving High Street. After negotiating a railway level crossing that was frequently shut to road vehicles, a driver had to manoeuvre through a carriageway which, in the early nineteen-fifties, was still being used by buses in both directions, even though parts of it were too narrow to allow them to pass each other.

*The Quay Railway about to enter West Quay Road.*

*The original Poole railway station at the side of the Towngate Street level crossing.*

*Removing the railway lines from West Quay Road, 1961.*

*The railway lines that ran through the Old Town between Poole Station and the Quay were a regular source of danger to traffic, particularly cyclists and motor-cyclists.*

*Looking down Commercial Road towards Ashley Cross just after the road had been widened.*

The borough council experimented with various one-way systems, which included diverting buses from Hamworthy along West Quay Road and into North Street, but none of the solutions was satisfactory or popular. The traders of High Street - and, indeed, many councillors - were unhappy with proposals to restrict parking or traffic using the road. Eventually an order was made to widen it to a uniform width of 40 feet, a solution much preferred to the one favoured by the planners, of building a new road from Poole Bridge to Longfleet.

Traffic proceeding from High Street to Hamworthy faced further obstacles. The landward side of the Quay was frequently obstructed by traders' stalls, and the harbour side by the railway lines, on which were the inevitable clutter of goods trucks. Despite many efforts, including raising the matter in Parliament, the Corporation could not even persuade British Rail to light the trucks at night. The quarrels were not resolved before the decision in 1960 to abandon the line, which ran to the Quay from Poole Station via Nile Row and West Quay Road. The track was taken up in 1961, the same year in which the new Poole Corporation Act finally gave the council the powers it needed to deal with obstructions caused by quayside traders.

One more hazard remained before a driver could finally reach Hamworthy, and that was Poole Bridge. When the first bridge was built, the merchants of Poole, whose livelihood depended upon shipping, insisted that sea traffic should always have right of way. Even a solitary yacht could still demand that the bridge was opened to let it pass. It was a right that could be amended only by a new Act of Parliament. As the quickest recorded time for the existing bridge to be opened to allow passage of a vessel was more than five and a quarter minutes - two minutes, ten seconds to raise, and three minutes, seven seconds to lower - it often caused serious delays. In 1962 there were 3,187 openings of Poole Bridge, an increase of 50 per cent on 1959. New statutory powers were desperately needed to deal with this situation.

In other parts of the town, the Corporation had more success in improving the driver's lot. It decided in 1958 that it was inequitable that traffic coming into Poole via Ringwood Road, and wishing to travel west, should be routed through residential areas of Oakdale before it could turn right from Dorchester Road into Wimborne Road and continue westward via Fleetsbridge. It decided to build a new road to link Ringwood Road to the Fleetsbridge roundabout.

The road was built roughly along the line of the Old Wareham Road, which had long since become impassable. Though there were still vestiges of a former road in places, there was also a huge bomb crater which all but prohibited even pedestrians from using it. In 1958 the council bought many plots of land along the proposed line of the road, and filled in low-lying areas with fly ash from Poole generating station. In June the following year, road-laying work was carried out by MEXE, the Government experimental engineering establishment at Christchurch, in co-operation with Rotary Hoes of Essex. MEXE considered it to be a valuable trial of its new methods and equipment. As one line of vehicles laid gravel, another consolidated it with cement, after which it was compacted into a level, smooth surface. The new roadway was laid at the rate of some 14 feet a minute, and consumed 200 tons of material and 70 tons of cement each hour. MEXE gave demonstrations of its new technique to members of the Royal Engineers and Southampton University, and to engineers from the United States and Canada. In the autumn, after the compacted surface had been covered with tar chippings, barriers were removed from each end, and the road was opened to traffic with no fuss or formality. The following year the Ministry of Transport accepted the road as a classified highway.

The Ministry was less happy, however, about accepting the 'give way to traffic on your right' advisory signs which since 1956 had been displayed at the approaches to Fleetsbridge roundabout, and ordered their removal. The signs had been erected at the suggestion of the council's Accident Prevention Sub-committee. It appeared that they had been generally welcomed and respected by motorists, and thus helped to reduce the number of accidents. The official view, however, was that the signs were in conflict with the Highway Code, which at that time declared that there were no rights of way, in general, at roundabouts, and that therefore, they could cause accidents, rather than prevent them.

The sub-committee and its energetic part-time road safety organiser, Victor Swatridge, a former Dorset police superintendent, launched a vigorous campaign to get the signs reinstated. Mr Swatridge gained the support of the South-West England Accident Prevention Federation, and it was discovered that other towns which had copied Poole's signs had not been ordered to remove them. They had also aroused interest in Jersey and South Africa. Official patience, however, was wearing thin, and Poole was threatened with the withdrawal of grants toward highway expenses unless the notices were promptly removed!

Other achievements of the council's Roads and Engineering Committee were less spectacular. It made heavy weather of its plans for a one-way gyratory system at Sandbanks, but eventually got its way. Fleets Lane was extended to connect with Fleetsbridge roundabout, but there was considerable delay over plans to widen the main A35 road to Bournemouth at Ashley Cross, where it narrowed dangerously. The only way in which it could be widened was by demolishing a number of shops in Commercial Road, on the eastern side of the junction, for which a compulsory purchase order was made. The shops were demolished when the order had been confirmed, but it was some time before the Ministry agreed that the road could be widened. The Corporation sold some of the surplus land as a site for a new parade of shops, and the rest was used to provide an off-street car park for Lower Parkstone.

The baleful influence of Dr Beeching's proposals for the future of British Rail began to cast its shadow over Poole in 1961, when rumours reached the borough council of plans for a total closure of a 30-mile section of line between Broadstone and Templecombe, and for ending the parcel delivery service from Poole station. Such a line closure would call into question the future of the Pines Express, which linked Poole with Manchester and Liverpool via the former Somerset and Dorset Railway line. Poole considered that the loss of the 'Pines' could seriously affect the borough's holiday trade from the north, as well as the number of visitors from other parts of Dorset.

All British Rail could be persuaded to say at that stage amounted to an admission that the economics of the line were under investigation. In 1962, Poole joined Blandford Borough and Rural Councils, and Sturminster Newton Rural District Council, in objecting to the closure of the Broadstone-Templecombe line. All efforts to save the route were in vain.

Less that a year later, on 8th September 1962, the Pines Express left Bournemouth West Station for Manchester, travelling for the last time via the old Somerset and Dorset line, before being re-routed via Southampton, Oxford and Birmingham. It was hauled by the 2-10-0 locomotive *Evening Star*, the last steam locomotive to be built by British Rail, which was completed at its Swindon works in 1950. Railway enthusiasts were out in force to see the express make its farewell visit to Poole station, bearing a wreath featuring the old Somerset and Dorset colours.

# Street Lighting

In 1953, most of Poole's roads were still the unmade-up, gaslit streets dating from before the second world war, and Government restrictions prevented anything but a gradual solution to the problem. However, each year the Borough Engineer's new lighting section was able to spend about £10,000 on converting gas lamps in existing highways to electric street lighting. By the end of 1962, all but 1,120 gas lamps had been replaced, and 6,350 electric lamps had been installed.

The increasing ownership of television sets, and in particular the great popularity of *Coronation Street*, created unexpected problems about switching the new lamps on and off. The Corporation had, in agreement with the electricity supply undertaking, installed a switching system by which all lights could be switched on from a central control room. It relied on an electrical pulse being transmitted down the supply lines. The effect of so many television sets being turned on at about the same time in the evening created a similar surge of electricity, with the result that street lamps could suddenly switch off after dark, or come on when it was still daylight! The Corporation had to abandon the system and instal timers.

*Gas standards at the Borough Engineer's depot near the Stadium. Early in the replacement programme, there was little demand for the old gas 'standards' even at a price of £2-10-0 (£2.50). Serpentine Road residents petitioned that the 'ugly posts' be taken away from their 'tidy street'.*

# Private Street Works

The Government also rationed the amount which could be spent on making up builders' gravelled roads with tarmac surfaces, drainage and street lighting. Although it was fully aware of the size of the borough council's problem, at most it allowed only some £70,000 a year to be spent on this work. That was one bar to speedy progress. Another was that even though residents were urging the Corporation to carry out the work, there could be long delays caused by appeals to the Magistrates' Court about some aspect of the scheme, or the amount of cost apportioned to frontagers. In 1962, for instance, Corporation staff spent 13 days in the Magistrates' Court dealing with appeals, and another two days at further appeals to Quarter Sessions.

Nevertheless, in the five years up to the end of 1962, sixteen miles of private roads had been made up by the Corporation, and a further nine miles built by developers. That still left a further 35 miles of private roads to be dealt with, and the council came under all kinds of pressure to change its priorities for private street works. There was nothing new about that, however. Many years earlier, the colourful Alderman Arthur Dacombe, himself a building contractor, made it his practice to finish any statement he made in the council chamber with the words '...and isn't it time, Mr Mayor, that Good Road was made a good road?'

Residents determined to get to the top of the list turned to the local Press to publicise the case for making up their street without further delay. Residents of Lake Road, Hamworthy, for instance, complained that it was full of nine-inch potholes and that buses serving Rockley Sands holiday camp were responsible for cracks in their ceilings. A midwife called to a birth in Oakdale was said to have had to abandon her car before she could reach the house, leaving the anxious father to fetch an oxygen cylinder. Creekmoor branded itself 'Poole's forgotten village,' partly on account of the state of its private streets, and residents picketed a council meeting with placards.

For residents of Sandy Lane, Upton, which ran along the line of a Roman road, the question of how and where to demand action was more complex. They felt that as the road had originally been built some 1,900 years earlier, it must surely qualify as an ancient highway, which by law it was the responsibility of the local authority to repair...but which authority? That was the first difficulty, for the road marked the western boundary of Poole and the eastern boundary of Wareham and Purbeck Rural District Council. The latter replied that their boundary stopped short of the road, at a ditch on its western side. Poole's view was that, however old the road might be, it was not an ancient highway within the meaning of the Private Street Works Act.

One frustrated resident declared that whether it belonged to Rome,

Wareham or Poole, the road still needed repair, a thought which may have prompted Mr D Coleman of Saint Peter's Close, Sandy Lane, to appeal to the Roads Department of the City of Rome. He wrote:

*None of the local authorities here will accept any responsibility for the upkeep...This road is part of one of the military roads, built by your soldiers during the conquest of Britain between the years 55 BC and 350 AD.*

*I have no doubt that during your occupation the road was kept in the same beautiful state of repair as all your roads - which, even today, are the only good highways we have in Britain, and I am sure you would be grieved to see how they have been neglected.*

*It occurs to me that under the UN Scheme for Technical Assistance, perhaps your country might make a grant, or, preferably, send a road-making team to the Dorset County Council to show them what should and could be done...*

Rome rose to the challenge. The following telegram was despatched to *The Mayor, Upton Village, Dorset*

*Relating to your request for technical assistance required to repair ancient Roman highway. If assistance still wanted, please advise me, whereupon will send special road engineer. Torqui, Minister, Public Works.*

## Coast Protection

To protect the beach at Sandbanks Recreation Ground, and to reclaim some of the sand lost during the second world war, Poole Corporation in 1953 constructed 15 groynes at a cost of £100,000.

In 1957 the Corporation acquired the necessary land to construct a promenade and sea wall that would link the promenade at Shore Road with the section that had been constructed along the sea frontage of Saint Ann's Hospital, Canford Cliffs, between 1952 and 1954. But there was considerable public opposition to the scheme, because it involved the removal of a local landmark, Simpson's Folly.

The Folly comprised the remains of a large concrete house constructed on the seafront by a Captain Simpson in about 1882. To unfamiliar eyes, it appeared to be no more than an enormous heap of masonry that obstructed one's way along the beach between Shore Road and Flaghead Chine: but it had already passed into local legend as a paradigm of the parable of the house built upon sand, or as an important example of Victorian concrete engineering.

*Simpson's Folly before it was blown up. Its protecting walls had been demolished by the sea and its foundations undermined.*

Others maintained that removing the Folly would spoil the relatively natural appearance of the seafront, and deprive it of a windbreak and an attractive place for sunbathing.

Objections to the Corporation's £77,500 scheme meant that a public inquiry had to be held in 1960, when a rather less romantic picture of the Folly's history was revealed. For a start, it was not built on sand, but upon a clay outcrop on the shore. The house, which took three or four years to complete, had been surrounded by concrete sea walls. 'The walls stood out, seeming to bid defiance to the waves of the roaring sea,' the *Poole Herald* of the day reported, but their defiance was short-lived. Captain Simpson lived in the house for only five weeks before he left it to the mercy of the elements, and of those members of the public who enjoyed looking round it and covering the walls with graffiti.

By 1890 the Corporation considered that the house was dangerously unstable, and called upon the then owner, the Reverend Hugh Pearson, to make it safe or demolish it. When he failed to do so, the task of demolition was given to the Borough Surveyor. The building was not perhaps as unstable as had been thought, however, for when three thirty-six-pound charges of gunpowder were detonated beneath its foundations, only part of it collapsed. A further explosion of the same size was needed to reduce it to a pile of enormous concrete blocks, the form in which it became known as Simpson's Folly.

At the public inquiry the Corporation argued that it was essential to get rid of the Folly in order to make the sea defences permanently safe and provide a level promenade for older people and others who did not wish to clamber over a mass of rubble more than twenty feet high. John Barron, the Borough Engineer, estimated that the Corporation could save £1,000 by using it as a source of 1,000 cubic yards of hardcore for the sea wall. He told the inquiry there was no evidence that the Folly had any appreciable effect upon the stability of the beach, and maintained that it was of only limited value as a windbreak.

Following the inquiry, the Corporation's scheme was approved, and work commenced early in 1961. Its completion meant that only one gap, of some 270 yards, remained in a continuous promenade from Shore Road to Branksome Chine.

The cliffs abutting this gap had been so eroded by the weather that they were unsafe and a danger to the public using the sandy beach below. A coast protection scheme was prepared to provide a connecting sea wall, cut back the cliffs to an angle of repose, and plant them. This would mean, though, that properties in Martello Park lost even more of their curtilage, and negotiations with the owners to surrender land were not easily concluded.

Owners of seafront property were naturally reluctant to surrender land or contribute to the cost of coast protection. A £15,000 scheme to build two groynes to protect a number of properties near the harbour entrance in Banks Road, Sandbanks, for which the Corporation considered that owners should contribute to the costs, was settled only after a public inquiry in 1960. The objectors maintained that they had already spent considerable sums on their own sea defences, which were adequate, and that the cause of more recent erosion was the bulldozing of the beach to clear the remains of anti-invasion defences erected during the second world war.

In 1960 the Corporation also drew up a programme for cliff stabilisation work at Branksome Chine, as the result of which it would be possible to increase the width of the promenade by six feet to twenty feet, and by 1963 considerable progress had been made in coast protection. Where new sea walls were built, the objective was to make the promenade wide enough to accommodate a line of beach chalets. By the end of 1962 the Corporation owned 549 beach chalets, giving an income of £18,600. A further 88 chalets were approved for construction on the new section of promenade then being built between Shore Road and Saint Ann's Hospital.

*(Above) Storms caused much damage to the coast prior to the coast protection works.*

*(Below) Coast Protection works in progress near Shore Road as seen from 'Little Fosters', Sir Bernard and Lady Docker's house.*

*Rubble from the remains of Simpson's Folly was used as hardcore to extend the Shore Road promenade.*

# Poole's Postal Address

In the nineteen-fifties, virtually the only district of Poole which had the word 'Poole' in its postal address was the Old Town. An earlier borough council, which had been consulted in 1933 on the Post Office's wish to amalgamate its Bournemouth and Poole offices, had decided it was useless 'to kick against the pricks.' With the demise of the Poole Post Office, the prospect of obtaining a 'Poole' postal address for the Branksome Park, Canford Cliffs, Sandbanks and Branksome districts, or for the 'Parkstone, Dorset' address to be changed, became even more remote.

In 1952 the council decided that the position was intolerable. It had mounted a deputation to the Postmaster-General, Lord de la Warr, demanding that he change these addresses to indicate they were in Poole. Although he was sympathetic, declaring it was important that a town the size of Poole should be correctly designated in all postal matters, he later wrote that, as there was no sorting office in the town large enough to deal with all Poole's mail, he was unable to grant its petition.

Poole Council then was made of sterner stuff than its predecessor in the nineteen-thirties. Its resolve to kick against the pricks was given added impulse when a BBC broadcast from Loewy Engineering's new factory in Poole was announced as coming from Bournemouth, and tenants on a new Poole council estate off Wallisdown Road were informed that their postal address was Bournemouth. The Member of Parliament, Captain Pilkington, raised the matter in the Commons and arranged a further meeting between members of the council and the Postmaster-General.

Captain Pilkington was told that the Postmaster-General would be willing to change the postal addresses, provided there was general agreement among the residents. Letters of opposition had been received from Branksome Park, Canford Cliffs and Sandbanks. The deputation was at least successful in getting the word 'Poole' introduced into the postal address of 17,000 residents of the borough who lived in areas south of Wallisdown Road. In 1956, 'Branksome, Bournemouth,' became 'Branksome, Poole,' and 'Parkstone, Dorset' became 'Parkstone, Poole, Dorset.' The Postmaster-General announced that because of strong local opposition elsewhere to a change of postal address, he would be unable to meet the council's wishes in other districts for the foreseeable future.

The council took another tack. In 1955 it called meetings with residents' associations in districts opposed to the change, and separately with the owners of the Branksome Tower, Sandbanks, Harbour Heights, Branksome Court and Haven Hotels. The hoteliers were intractable. They averred that a 'Bournemouth' address was a most valuable asset to their business, and that they would never voluntarily surrender it.

Still not satisfied, the council demanded another meeting with the new Postmaster-General, Dr Charles Hill, the former 'Radio Doctor,' who had dispensed popular and homely advice on health matters during the war. Poole's case was that there would be great benefits to the borough from a uniform postal address, but that if Dr Hill wished to appease the hoteliers, who were leading the opposition, the Corporation would accept that the hotels could retain their 'Bournemouth' address.

It seemed an unlikely ploy, but it worked. The avuncular Dr Hill listened patiently to the deputation's arguments. Then, in his deep Father Christmas voice, and best bedside manner, he assured its members that while he sympathised greatly with them, the Post Office could not overrule the expressed wishes of the residents. He was sure, though, he said comfortingly, that the council would eventually have its way.

In 1960 the council tried yet another tack. It asked the head postmaster of the Bournemouth-Poole district for an appointment. He 'reluctantly' agreed to receive a deputation in May that year, to consider postal districts, and it took him until November to give his decision. He had looked into the matter thoroughly, he reported, and it would cost the Post Office an extra £300 a year to grant the council's wish to change the postal addresses of Branksome Park, Canford Cliffs and Sandbanks. This extra cost could not be justified.

The council considered the decision outrageous, when in the same year the Post Office was mounting a campaign exhorting everyone to use the correct postal address. In December 1960, when he officially opened Poole Joint Head Post Office in High Street, the Mayor, Alderman Bill Cole, declared that Poole should have its own head Post office and postmark, and not share them with Bournemouth. The High Street office had been closed since 1958 for reconstruction, after the sorting office had been moved to new premises at Sterte. Approximately 180,000 letters a week were posted in the borough, and 259,000 delivered, by a team of 90 postmen and women employed at Poole's two delivery offices.

It was not until February 1961 that a council deputation was able to attend the Postmaster-General's office once again. It consisted of Aldermen Butler, Lloyd-Allen, and Stokes, and the Town Clerk. Two councillors - Geoffrey Adams of Branksome Park, Canford Cliffs and Sandbanks, and Robert Hann of Broadstone - had asked to be removed from it. Mr Hann told the council: 'We want *Broadstone, Dorset* - and we are going to keep it.'

The portents did not seem good, for the deputation found that the matter had been delegated to the Assistant Postmaster-General, Miss Mervyn Pike, MP, but it went ahead and put its case. It was not just a matter of local pride, the members argued, but one of business, as well as misrepresentation. Urgent police messages arising in the seaside areas of Poole were often sent to the Hampshire force. Important correspondence for Poole's Medical Officer of Health, and solicitors' requests to the Town Clerk for searches to be made in the local registry, were frequently delayed by being sent to their opposite numbers in Bournemouth. In any case, the council questioned the earlier assertions that there was strong local opposition to the change of address.

For the first time, a Poole deputation felt it was not being patronised on this issue. Miss Pike expressed genuine sympathy with its arguments. In fact, she remarked, she had an aunt who lived in Canford Cliffs, and had never been able to convince her that she did not live in Bournemouth. The deputation came away from the meeting happier than its predecessors.

In July, Miss Pike wrote to the Town Clerk: 'I will be candid with you. The problem has placed me in a dilemma. On the one hand there was strong opposition from the residents in 1956...and we are always reluctant to change an address unless we are satisfied that we shall have the support of the people concerned.' But in the light of the assurance she had been given, that 'Poole' would be more acceptable than 'Westbourne, Bournemouth,' provided the name of the district - Branksome Park, Canford Cliffs or Sandbanks - was also included in the address, she was inclined to grant Poole's request. A senior official assured the Town Clerk: 'The postal services in these areas would not suffer materially from the change in address.'

As requested by Miss Pike, the council circulated her letter to the press, broadcasting and television organisations, and members of the public were invited to write to her with their views. All the residents of Sandbanks were anonymously provided with postcards, already addressed and requiring only a signature, on which to express their opposition. Although the Canford Cliffs Land Society declared that it was neutral on the issue, the Branksome Park Association voted against any change, and success for the council seemed unlikely.

The council was therefore delighted when, in September 1961, Miss Pike wrote to say there had been little opposition to the proposed change of address, and that arrangements would be made to bring it into effect in February 1962. 'It's dogged that does it!'

Some disgruntled residents, however, were disinclined to take defeat lying down. The Branksome Park Association protested to the Post Office that its letter had been taken as representing only one view, not that of the majority of its members. It claimed that 532 residents in Branksome Park were against the change, and only 67 in favour, and that the total number of opponents rose to 877 when responses from Canford Cliffs and Sandbanks residents were included. At the annual meeting of Branksome Park, Canford Cliffs, Lilliput and Sandbanks branch of Poole Conservative Association, the Member of Parliament (who had received a knighthood in the 1961 New Year Honours List) was warned that his attitude over the postal address controversy could cost the party votes. Despite shouts of protest when he maintained that the majority of people in the area wanted the address changed, Sir Richard Pilkington was unperturbed. He said he was not prepared to do anything about continued opposition to it, 'because I have been on three deputations asking for that very thing. I am pro-Poole every time.'

*'The Branksome Park Association feels very strongly that Branksome Park should remain 'Bournemouth West' and not 'Poole, Dorset' although my husband and I would prefer otherwise'*

*Secretary of the Branksome Park Association, 1961.*

*'There are still 9 postwomen at Parkstone'*

*Poole Herald, December 1956.*

*Weston's Lane off High Street was one of the more commodious of Poole's many Lanes. It led off the eastern side of High Street. Weston House and the Hermitage lay behind the gate on which the Jolliffe family emblems had been erected. The Hermitage had housed Poole's first hospital but both buildings, after years of use as tenements, had become derelict.*

## Slum Clearance

In 1955 the Government announced that it would consider approving schemes to clear the country's slums. The Corporation's public health inspectors, who were already familiar with the problem of unfit houses, reported that there were 797 such properties in the town, about one in twenty of its housing stock. In 1956 the borough council agreed a five-year programme to clear all the slums of the town and rehouse the displaced families. The scheme received Ministerial approval in the same year.

All but about a hundred of the town's slum dwellings were in the Old Town. Those outside the Old Town could be dealt with relatively simply by clearance orders, which after the rehousing of the tenants and demolition of the building, left the owner able to sell or redevelop the cleared site.

It was quite another problem with the slums of the Old Town. The obsolete road network, with its narrow lanes and alleyways, was stifling the town centre. High Street, its main artery, narrowed in parts to sixteen feet; Lagland Street, the secondary road, narrowed to less than twenty feet at its southern end; and Strand Street, which connected the two, had a width varying between twelve and fourteen feet. It was therefore decided that a new lateral road would have to be built, and a new route for traffic between Poole Bridge and Longfleet; and that other roads would be widened or closed. To do so meant that not only had the sites of slum houses to be bought, but also commercial properties, and even fit houses which were intermingled with the slums. Each slum clearance order was therefore accompanied by a compulsory purchase order, authorising the council to purchase all the land required.

By the time public health and building inspectors had completed their careful inspections, the number of slum properties had risen to 987. The council began its programme at the Quay end of the Old Town, and by the end of 1962 it had made 55 slum clearance orders comprising 873 properties. Public inquiries into each of these orders had been held, and most of them had

*King Street was planned to disappear completely in the reconstruction. It ran from West Street to join Market Street just above the Guildhall. The photograph shows the side wall of Rogers Almshouses, then two almshouses followed by the Gaol and House of Correction which housed a room for the detention of debtors and contained a treadmill. Just out of the photograph was the fire station and on the opposite side of the road had been the Poole Court of Record.*

*Wellington House. Market Street, was at the end of King Street opposite the old Greyhound Hotel. The plaque commemorated the fact that Thomas Bell, FRCS, had been born in the house in 1792. The house was later converted into the Duke of Wellington public house. After being used for some years as a shop it had then reverted to use as two private houses.*

been approved. Despite the inevitable delays in arranging inquiries, and the time needed for the Minister to consider each case, and for the Corporation to purchase the premises, nearly six hundred families had been rehoused by the end of 1962.

With a new road pattern to be put into place and sewerage, water, electricity and gas services to be relayed or renewed, there were, necessarily, delays in being able to build accommodation in the Old Town. This meant that cleared areas often remained unused. They were referred to locally as 'bomb sites' and the council was accused of having done to Poole what Hitler failed to do! On the other hand, if the old premises were not quickly demolished, they were taken over by squatters, to the great irritation of those living nearby.

There were, too, the inevitable human dramas which such a large operation caused. In the early years, the dispossessed families usually had to be rehoused away from the Old Town, on one of the Corporation's new housing estates, where they felt cut off from their friends. One tenant complained to the local newspaper that she had spent Christmas in her new house *'and it was Hell!'* The paper solicited the views of other rehoused families, whom they referred to as the 'Outspan Tenants.'

There were many other human problems. Many of the residents of the Old Town still lived in the house where they had been born, and which was now regarded as a slum. This proved to them that their homes need not be condemned, and they wished to be left to die in them. Mr Charles Kelly was not alone in challenging the council to knock the house down around him. He told a reporter that the walls were damp, the ceiling was peeling, and there was no toilet, but it was near his work and '*we use the Old Orchard Car Park conveniences.*'

By the end of 1962 it had been possible to rehouse some of the 'Outspan' tenants who still wished to return to the Old Town. The Corporation had not been able to complete its five-year programme within that period, but it was well on the way to doing so.

*A view from Strand Street. The building being demolished is the Rising Sun in Castle Street. Once the most important hostelry in Poole, most of it had been converted into living units. The buildings shown as still standing to the left of the photograph are the Salvation Army's Citadel and, to its left, No 27 Castle Street.*

*Looking down Castle Street after the demolition of the Rising Sun. No 27 Castle Street is shown on the right. It was once the home and offices of Robert Parr, the infamous Town Clerk of Poole, 1833-1836.*

*(Above) Demolition in Market Street, at the rear of St. Mary's Roman Catholic Church, West Quay Road.*

*(Left) Small traders, such as this general store on the corner of Lagland Street and Weston's Lane, found it hard to survive the loss of customers caused by slum clearance.*

*(Right) Properties awaiting clearance in the Old Town were used for Army and Civil Defence training exercises. A 'casualty' awaits collection on a neighbour's doorstep: but it is Dick Poole, the Evening Echo reporter, who gets a cup of tea!*

82

*Gray's Yard, Lagland Street, which included Nos. 23, 25 and 27 Lagland Street. The stone sink and water tap at the end of the courtyard served the three houses.*

*Just behind the Guildhall in Hill Street was the Temperence Hall built in1860. In the 1950's it was used for a time by Butler's store but was derelict by 1960 and later demolished.*

*Lagland Street. Houses included in Clearance Area No.10.*

*Looking into the picturesque Castle Street from Strand Street.*

*(Above) Slum clearance and redevelopment meant that many Old Town families faced the prospect of moving to a new home - and in some cases eviction by private landlords. (Top left) Plan accompanying Clearance Area No. 7 showing all the properties in photograph below. The Minister held a public inquiry in May 1957 and confirmed that the properties in Castle Street could be compulsorly acquired as slums and that the non-residential properties, shown shaded on the plan, could be acquired for redevelopment.*

*Ridout's butchery shop, on the corner of Avenue Place, in its prosperous days.*

*Demolition and clearance between Avenue Place and High Street, 1962. Ridout's butchery business had lost its customers.*

# The Health of Poole

Prior to the passage of the National Health Service Act, 1946, there were five hospitals in Poole, but only one general purpose hospital, the Cornelia and East Dorset Hospital, whose name was soon changed to Poole General Hospital. The other Poole hospitals were specialist ones, such as the Corporation's Alderney Hospital for Infectious Diseases; Saint Ann's, a convalescent home for mental patients; Parkstone Sanatorium at Castle Hill for tuberculosis sufferers, and Saint Mary's for the old and chronically ill.

In 1947, responsibility for the hospitals was transferred to the South East Metropolitan Hospital Board, which was split in 1959, when Poole's hospitals came under the Wessex Regional Hospital Board, whose members were appointed by the Government and the professional societies.

Without an obviously accessible body or person to refer to, local complaints were frequently aired in the Press, which regularly reported on the number of patients awaiting surgery and on the time it took to be seen by a consultant. Demands on the hospital service, and its ever rising cost, were already a national problem. In Poole in the nineteen-fifties, problems were increased by an expanding population, and there was great public pressure for adequate hospital services. The borough council involved itself in the pressure and mounted several deputations to the Minister of Health, sometimes accompanied by representatives of the Hospital Management Committee, to urge the building of a new and larger hospital.

*Saint Ann's Hospital, Canford Cliffs.*

*The main entrance to the old Cornelia Hospital, Longfleet Road.*

*Alderman Geoffrey Bravery.*

*Poole Hospital had a flourishing League of Friends and regularly invited distinguished guests to address its annual meetings, held in the Conference Room at the Municipal Buildings. The speaker in 1955 was Lord Beveridge, one of the architects of the Welfare State.*

*Cornelia Hospital celebrated its golden jubilee in 1957, when this picture of senior staff, including the Matron, Miss Maud Welford (centre) was taken.*

*Accompanied by the Matron, Miss Frances Potts, and Ald. P G Templeman, Chairman of the Bournemouth and East Dorset Hospital Management Committee, HRH Princess Alexandra meets staff of Poole Hospital during her visit in 1961.*

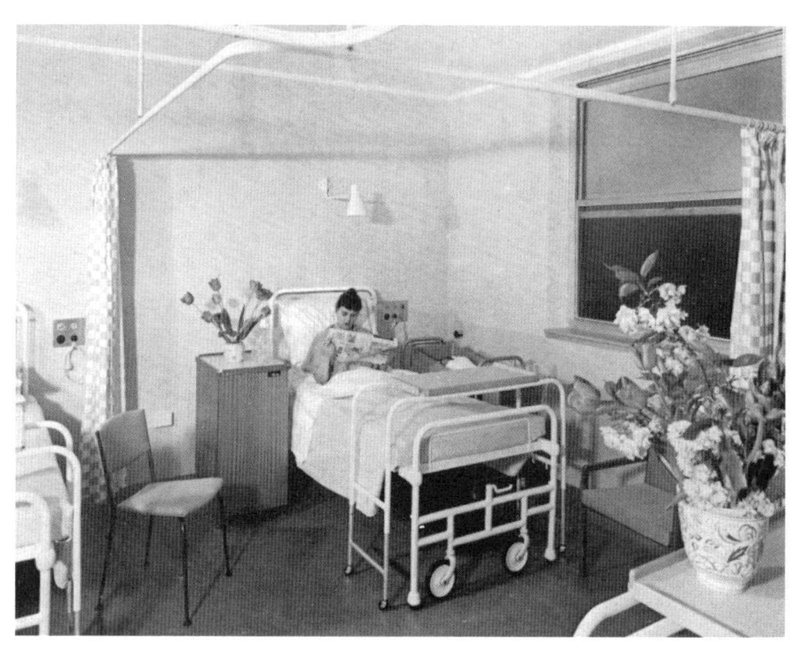

*A four-bedded ward in the new Maternity Wing.*

It was not, however, until 1956 that any deputation was given any hope of early action. The Minister told the deputation he hoped soon to be able to sanction the preparation of plans to build a detached Maternity Wing of a proposed new hospital in Poole.

Even so, work was not commenced on the new wing until 1959, and it was 1961 before it was completed. In May that year HRH the Princess Alexandra of Kent formally declared the building open at an impressive ceremony, at which the Royal Marines Band of HMS Daedalus played and the Bishop of Salisbury led prayers of dedication.

By this time, Poole had further good news. In the interim between the beginning of work on the maternity wing and the Princess's visit, the Minister had authorised the building of the first stage of a new Poole Hospital. This announcement had come in time for a start to be made on the new hospital, so that the Princess was able to lay its foundation stone after opening the maternity wing.

*Lord Rockley, Ald. P G Templeman, Chairman of the Bournemouth & East Dorset Hospital Management Committee and Ald. G Bravery, Vice-Chairman.*

# Personal Health & Welfare Services

The Personal Health and Welfare Services which had been previously carried out by Poole Borough Council were transferred to Dorset County Council by the National Health Service Act, 1946, leaving the Corporation responsible for only the environmental health service of the town.

However, in 1961, the county council delegated back to the Corporation most of the personal health and welfare services, which were mainly concerned with the health and welfare of mothers, children and the elderly.

Among these was the responsibility for providing sufficient qualified midwives to attend women at home during pregnancy, childbirth, and afterwards. In 1961, despite the opening of the new Maternity Wing at the hospital, 726 babies were delivered at home by the Health Department's thirteen midwives, and it was these midwives who held regular ante-natal, mothercraft and relaxation classes at the town's clinics, as well as child welfare clinics, where, in the early years, dried milk, cod liver oil and orange juice were distributed for children. It was desirable to have clinics reasonably near to patients' homes, and there were seven such clinics on the completion of the Layton Road clinic in Parkstone in 1961.

*Layton Road Clinic.*

Five doctors were then employed by the Corporation, whose duties included medically inspecting children four times during their school life. If any problem was found, a child was usually referred to one of the Health Department's clinics, or to hospital or a family doctor. The department operated minor ailment, dental, speech and asthma clinics, as well as an audiology unit. Its doctors were also responsible for immunising and inoculating children against poliomyelitis, diphtheria, whooping cough, tetanus and smallpox, unless parents wished their family doctor to be responsible.

In the nineteen-forties poliomyelitis, previously thought of as infantile paralysis, began to infect older children and even adults. Its growing prevalence in the nineteen-fifties became very worrying to the Health Department, as it was not known exactly how it was transmitted, and there was no specific cure. In 1955, for instance, there were sixteen confirmed cases in Poole Of eleven patients who developed paralysis, three died. The Medical Officer of Health suspected that bathing in the sea might be the cause, and at one time even suggested that the habit of shaking hands should be abandoned, to stop the spread of infection. But by 1958, immunisation against the disease was possible, and school doctors gave 15,000 injections to protect children. Only four cases were reported the following year.

There still remained, however, the problem of those who had already been paralysed, and the town's medical officers actively encouraged the building of the Spastics Centre on land provided by the council in Langside Avenue, Wallisdown. Dr D S Parken, deputy medical officer of health, helped to launch an appeal for £5,500 towards the cost of the work.

The fifteen Health Visitors employed by the Corporation assisted the medical officers in their visits to schools. They were responsible for ensuring that any problems found by the doctors were dealt with, and they visited children under five years old, expectant mothers, tuberculosis patients and problem families in their homes.

In addition, the Corporation employed eighteen District Nurses who, at the request of the hospital or general practitioners, visited patients in their homes. They were qualified to give injections and change dressings under the direction of the doctor, as well as to prepare patients for admission to hospital and attend on them, if necessary, after they were discharged. In 1961 the Home Nursing Service made nearly 50,000 visits to patients in their homes.

To help single-parent families, mainly widowed, single, separated and divorced women who needed to work to support their children, the Corporation operated a purpose-built day nursery in the grounds of Belmont Court, Parkstone, which provided fifty places for children between two and five years of age. The Corporation made a charge for this service unless it created financial hardship.

A charge was made, too, for its Home Help service, which employed about eighty part-time Home Helps. They could take over household duties such as preparing children for school, cooking, cleaning, washing and shopping, in households which needed such help because of pregnancy, illness or infirmity.

The borough council's Health Committee also controlled the Port Health Service as well as refuse collection and disposal. In 1961, with a population of just over 90,000, some 25,000 tons of refuse were dealt with at a cost of just under £100,000, less £20,000 received for salvage.

It was important to centralise the administration of the borough's health service, and to provide a further clinic to serve the south-east area of the town. The Central Clinic was therefore built as part of the evolving Civic Centre on the corner of Sandbanks Road and Park Road. It accommodated the Medical Officer of Health's staff, including the environmental services operated by public health inspectors. It was also possible to establish a dental surgery for children and expectant mothers, and to hold clinical sessions for the south-east area of the borough, thereby allowing other temporary premises to be released.

The Corporation employed seven public health inspectors, who were responsible for the sanitary condition of the town. Their responsibilities included the water supply, drainage, sewerage, food supplies and food premises, infectious diseases, industrial hygiene and atmospheric pollution. During the period their housing responsibilities were particularly heavy, because of slum clearance. They had to satisfy a Ministry inspector that each property included by the borough council in a clearance order was properly categorised as a slum dwelling.

*The Central Clinic under construction.*

# Industry and Commerce

A list of the leading industrial manufacturers in Poole during the middle of the nineteen-fifties would have included several old established firms that owed their origins to local enterprise, needs, or resources. But among the largest and best known would have been a number of nationally important companies that had moved into the borough for a variety of reasons - such as relocation because of the war - and subsequently prospered.

Poole's most successful companies were in general doing so well, despite the sombre national outlook, that a local newspaper was proclaiming 'Poole's industrial boom,' even though the Government had deleted most of the land designated for industrial expansion by Poole Corporation. The Government's view was that with unemployment in Poole so low - it totalled 92 men and 63 women in 1955 - the town was unlikely to get approval for new industry.

Among leading firms with strong local roots were Poole Pottery, and British Seagull, the outboard motor manufacturer. In 1953, Seagull took over premises at Fleetsbridge from C H Gould, an independent radio and electrical dealer. Advertisements for Gould's Radio House of Poole usually featured a photograph of Cyril Gould, its larger than life proprietor, projecting sound advice down the telephone to an imaginary customer. Then there were firms such as Hamworthy Engineering, started in a small workshop on the Hamworthy quayside by two brothers in 1914, or Bluebird Caravans, founded in Poole in 1940, and presided over by Mr Bill Knott, another of the town's more colourful businessmen. Hamworthy invested £60,000 in extensions to its quayside works in 1953, followed over the next few years by the building of new premises at Fleetsbridge, and a foundry at Mannings Heath. Bluebird by 1955 had a workforce of 350 at its Newtown factory, and in 1958, it was publicly floated, with Mr Knott retaining 51 per cent of the 175,000 shares, which were priced at 14s 3d (71.25p).

Among Poole's nationally known companies, Ryvita, the crispbread manufacturer, advertised its products as coming 'From Poole to the World.' Its managing director boasted that Poole could produce Ryvita and ship it to Australia more cheaply than it could be produced there. A few years later, he was appointed managing director of the Australian factory! By 1954 British Drug Houses, then the town's largest employer, was also the largest manufacturer of laboratory chemicals in Europe, and its profits were soaring. Chalwyn Lamps, manufactured at Newtown, were known all over the world, especially in Africa. The firm's exports were worth £2 million a year. In the later nineteen-fifties Chalwyn expanded its Newtown factory, only to find that sales of its hurricane lamps dropped dramatically as a result of competition from

*Bolson's shipbuilding yard on the West Shore, seen from the site of Christopher Hill's grain silo in West Quay Road.*

cheaper lamps. W L Miller and Sons also claimed a national market with the slogan 'You'll go a lot further on Millers' pies and sausages,' accompanied by a picture of a jolly, well-nourished family rolling along the highway in a car constructed almost entirely from such products.

Nearly 300 planning applications a month were being received by the borough council, another sign of a prospering economy. There were plans by Millers to build an abattoir at their Sterte food factory, while J Bolson and Son sought to reclaim land from Holes Bay to extend their shipbuilding yard in West Quay Road. In 1958 Bolsons built the suction dredger *Sand Grebe*, which was said to be the largest ship yet built in Poole. The growing popularity of television brought more orders for Sydney S Bird and Sons, manufacturers of radio and television tuners and other electronic equipment. The company moved to Poole from Enfield in 1953, and by the end of the decade it was employing 1,200 people in a factory of 100,000 square feet at Fleets Lane. One attractive feature of Poole's industrial landscape, from the point of view of larger companies, was the considerable number of engineering companies in the area which could undertake sub-contract work when required.

Unemployment in Poole increased to 296 men and 155 women in 1956, in the recession brought about by the Suez crisis. Yet the temporary reintroduction of petrol rationing as the result of that débacle did not discourage F English Limited from going ahead with ambitious plans for new car showrooms, workshops and a filling station in Poole Road. This development was the first to breach the high brick wall, about one mile long, that extended to County Gates from near the corner of Saint Aldhelm's Road, and divided the Branksome Park residential area from the rest of Branksome. The company purchased three large properties that lay behind the wall, followed by a fourth, on to which it soon expanded.

English's near neighbours in Poole Road, Southernprint Limited, completed the development of their newspaper and periodical printing plant, delayed until 1958 by Government building restrictions. Originally known as the Times-Herald Building, it was begun in 1949 by Bournemouth Times Limited. As well as owning and publishing the *Bournemouth Times, Poole and Dorset Herald* and other local newspapers, the company won contracts to print an increasing number of nationally known magazines and periodicals. It was purchased in 1953 by Southern Newspapers, publishers of the *Bournemouth Daily Echo* and other evening newspapers at Southampton and Weymouth, after James Putnam, the proprietor, hinted that he might be prepared to sell to one of the national newspaper groups, such as Thomson, which were busily investing in the regional press. At Newtown in 1958, British Drug Houses planned large new warehouses and offices in Broom Road. Northey Rotary Compressors had established a factory in Alder Road. In the Old Town, Wessex Industries had taken over the old Dolphin Brewery and were making fork-lift trucks for

*Signs of industrial revival in Market Street, 1960.*

British Rail and many other customers. The company demolished a property in Market Street, and converted another into a showroom, as its sales increased.

By 1959, the Medical Officer of Health reported, there were 400 factories in the town. The usual concomitants of such expansion - more retail premises, complaints about industrial pollution, and takeovers by larger conglomerates - did in due course emerge, but there was little immediate prospect of major improvements to the shopping facilities in the town centre. Beales, a family-run department store in Bournemouth, and one of the flagships of the neighbouring borough's retail supremacy, opened its first Poole shop, which sold mainly bedding, at the Longfleet end of High Street, in 1955. Butlers' department store, on the corner of High Street and North Street, was taken over and revitalized by Arthur Newbery Limited in 1959. But in 1957, the same year that Poole's first supermarket, Fine Fare, made its appearance in Kingland Crescent, the borough council received a somewhat discouraging report on prospects for retail expansion from its consultants, Goddard and Smith.

As regards pollution, these complaints often centred upon the town's two major power producers. Following conversion of the generating station boilers from coal to oil firing in 1957, Hamworthy residents had to endure oily smoke, and corrosive smuts tainted with sulphuric acid, which it was claimed ruined clothing, paintwork and garden produce. Heavy fallout in 1959, following problems with boiler tubes and burners, led to a partial shutdown. At an angry

*Poole Generating Station in its heyday, after conversion to oil firing.*

public meeting, a young woman confronted the station superintendent, Mr C J Stockell, with a new coat. *'I saved nine months to get this. Look at it now. Five minutes in Blandford Road and it's ruined,'* she told him, as the audience cheered. Mr Stockell admitted that there was 'a general lack of know-how' on the design of oil-fired equipment of that size, and that modifications might be necessary. These were later carried out at a cost of £24,000, and by February 1960 the borough council was informed that discharges of smuts had fallen to negligible proportions.

There were also complaints of dust and fumes from the Southern Gas Board's works, which, following the closure of some twenty smaller works, supplied gas to 132,000 consumers in an area of about 1,300 square miles. It was the largest surviving gasworks in the board's area, carbonising 230,000 tons of coal a year. The Corporation in 1950 had established five atmospheric pollution stations to measure the three main causes of air pollution. The results from its station in Park Lake Road gave it great concern. Although soot pollution decreased slightly in the period 1954-60, the fall-out of ash and grit, and sulphur trioxide and dioxide, increased alarmingly. In 1954, the yearly grit fall-out had been measured at 90 tons per square mile. In 1960 it was 170 tons. In 1954 the amount of sulphur compounds (which, combining with moisture in the air, produced sulphuric acid) was 95 tons. In 1960 it was measured at 125 tons.

Dr A E Haffner, the board's chief engineer, valiantly insisted that thanks to vigilance and good housekeeping, dust emissions outside the works were broadly no worse than in any other urban area: but the borough council was more concerned about the amount of coal dust blowing into its open-air swimming bath in Park Lake Road. There was so much dust that it was possible to scoop a scum off the water, claimed Alderman Donald Haynes, chairman of the Health Committee. A round table conference on the nuisance from dust and fumes was called between representatives of the board, the borough council and the Alkali Inspectorate.

The Gas Board had promised in 1958 to do away with the overhead ropeway which since 1924 had carried buckets of coal between its south and north works, but in 1961 it had second thoughts about replacing it with an enclosed conveyor, and removing the unattractive bridges that took the ropeway across South Road and Green Road. There was consternation at proposals to transport coal by lorry instead. In 1963 there were still complaints of 'filth' and 'tarry matter' getting into Poole Park Lake, but plans were in hand to construct a pumping station and rising main to intercept discharges from the gasworks - which the board claimed it was by law allowed to make into public sewers.

Poole's industries did not escape the takeover fever that gripped the City following the setting up in 1958 of the European Economic Community under the Treaty of Rome; but two more of the highly individual characters still to be

*The gasworks aerial coal conveyor.*

*An old wall-mounted gas lamp bracket in an alleyway off High Street*

found in the local business community were already in the vanguard of such developments. They were Edward Webster, a brilliant, plain-speaking engineer, and Leonard Matchan, a sharp-witted accountant, who had also been a Labour councillor and Parliamentary candidate for Poole. They met during the second world war through a mutual friend in the Home Guard, and pooled their knowledge of engineering and the cosmetics industry in Edward Webster Limited. Its West Howe factory produced lipstick containers by the million - one for practically every lipstick sold in Britain. Mr Webster, however, was in no danger of suffering the same fate as the managing director of Ryvita when he claimed that his company could also export lipstick containers to the United States and undercut local producers!

In 1956 the company acquired a Stock Exchange listing by a merger with Cope, Allman and Company Limited, a Birmingham manufacturer. It then launched on a breathtaking programme of acquisition and diversification that embraced companies in Britain, France, West Germany, and South Africa. In 1961, when he reported that profit was up by 45 per cent, and net asset value by 75 per cent, and recommended a 25 per cent dividend, Mr Matchan was looking to further expansion in India and Russia. As he drove the Cope, Allman group on to a stock market valuation of some £5 million, its empire of some three dozen companies came to embrace a vast range of products, from fire engine bells to Formula I racing cars and bespoke fishing tackle, as well as H & A Burden and Company, a long established ship chandlery business on Poole Quay that had once belonged to the Jolliffe family.

Another local businessman with a strong and forceful personality was at the helm of Christopher Hill Limited, the agricultural merchant and feed manufacturer, which was granted planning permission to erect a grain handling plant on the Quay, a short distance from Burdens. Constructed from four thousand tons of continuously poured concrete by a revolutionary sliding shutter process, the building rose to two-thirds of its final height of 85 feet in less than a week during November 1959. It was only the second completely new building on the Quay in this century, and quite unlike any other.

Christopher Hill Limited had been in business on the Quay since 1846, and had spread to a number of other sites in the Old Town. The chairman, Archie Hunt, an old boy of Poole Grammar School, whose father was twice Mayor of Poole, had worked for the firm since 1920, becoming managing director in 1936. Churchillian in manner and turn of phrase, he was proud of the fact that between then and 1963, it formed or acquired nearly a dozen subsidiary companies, and the turnover increased more than a hundredfold. By the end of 1962 the company had also built another grain silo, more than 90 feet high, in West Quay Road, and accepted a £1.5 million bid in cash and shares to become part of the Ranks Hovis McDougall group.

*The silo was built by a 'sliding shutter' method involving the continuous pouring of concrete through a platform raised by hydraulic jacks as the shell of the building emerged below.*

The takeover bid was one of two announced during the summer of 1962. Hamworthy Engineering went to the Powell Duffryn group for £3 million, amid talk of doubling the 1,000 strong workforce within the next few years. Two other old established quayside names, J R Wood and Company, and Hamworthy Coal Company, lost their individual identity as they were merged with other fuel distributors in the Associated Coal and Wharf group of companies to form Corrall Limited. Loewy Engineering, which had established itself in Branksome Park during the war, moving to purpose-built premises at Wallisdown in 1953, had been taken over in 1960 by Tube Investments. It had orders worth £3 million in 1961 from Europe, the Commonwealth and Japan for its metal forming machinery. In 1962 it supplied the biggest aluminium plate mill in western Europe and received a £2 million order for ball-bearing plant from Japan.

The Wallis Tin Stamping Company, whose founder had played a leading role in Poole's industrial revival, was taken over by the Metal Box Company. Colonel Wallis was head of the Poole Industrial Advisory Committee, set up shortly after the second world war to advise the Corporation on industrial matters. This connection between the borough council and industry was continued afterward by many Poole firms which each year invited the newly-elected mayor and mayoress to visit their factories. It led, also, to the staging of a 'Poole Can Make It' exhibition in Poole Park in 1948, at which 56 local firms displayed their products and advised on the skills required for work in their factories. Wallis Tin had factories at Hamworthy and in Bournemouth Road, Parkstone, which made shell cases and other armaments during the war. Post-war production included milk coolers and silent refrigerators, but its major product of metal closures was so successful that it soon became the only one. The company supplied millions of bottle caps for most of Europe's major food producers, and opened a new factory at Sterte, where production was concentrated following the takeover.

A five-week strike for trade union recognition by 500 employees at Bluebird Caravans in 1962, during which Mr Knott talked of switching 40 per cent of production to Germany, began after workers had been notified of a 20 per cent cut in wages. In August 1963 the company was merged with Sprite Caravans of Newmarket, in a share exchange deal worth £1.5 million. The new group was expected to control about half the £7 million a year caravan market. Mr Knott retired as managing director.

Unemployment had increased in Poole during 1962, as part of a national trend, but by the following summer there were many unfilled vacancies, particularly for women assembly workers, at firms such as Sydney Bird and Edward Webster. Millers' food factory was 'crying out' for women and girls, who could earn £7.16s a week at 21.

In 1960, Cyril Carter, president of Poole and District Chamber of Commerce, declared that although Poole was a go-ahead borough, it could not make up its mind whether to be an industrial centre or a holiday resort. In time, it was to succeed in both roles.

*Christopher Hill's silo in West Quay Road under construction.*

*'Not a single skilled worker in Poole is out of work.'*

*Poole Herald, 1954.*

*'On occasions there is bound to be voltage and frequency reductions.'*

*Electricity Board, September 1954.*

*'I am willing to wager that Poole will never achieve County Borough Status'*

*A C Templeman, Deputy Clerk to the Dorset County Council.*

*'Bill' Cole*

# Looking to the Future

## The Poole Corporation Bill

In Poole in the early nineteen-fifties the impression was abroad that great things lay in store for the town. Yet the feeling also remained that its civic leaders in Victorian times had parted with too much, too cheaply. Their greatest betrayal had been not to opt to become a county borough, as the County of the Town of Poole had the right to do under the local government reforms of 1888, but instead to allow Dorset County Council to assume some of the borough council's powers.

This feeling could recur every time a rate demand arrived, for the bill inevitably included a very substantial precept from Dorset County Council. This in time began to raise suspicions in the minds of some Poole citizens and civic leaders that, as well as being subservient to a predominantly rural county, in several key areas of local administration, the borough was also partially subsidizing it. Whether or not this was so - and figures were bandied about on both sides of the debate which sought to prove matters either way - it was also inevitable that a divide would open between the outlook of an expanding urban area such as Poole and the more sedate view of life generally taken at County Hall.

It was a feeling that could also arise when a queue of vehicles was delayed by the notorious hand-wound level crossing gates that bisected both High Street and Towngate Street, or traffic was delayed by the railway line that ran down West Quay Road and along the Quay. It now seemed that considerable sacrifices had been made for the sake of a railway connection into the town centre from Bournemouth, in addition to the one that had already been achieved via Wimborne to the rest of the network.

Great hopes had been raised by the recommendation of the Boundary Commission in 1945 that Poole should be made a county borough, but these were dashed by the Government's decision to abolish the Commission. Despite promises that there would be new proposals for the reform of local government, it meant that in the meantime, Poole would continue to be treated in the same way as a borough of only some three or four thousand inhabitants, and assumed to have insufficient resources or population to provide its own local services.

Dorset County Council had recognised this anomaly by delegating back to the borough council most of its education, planning and public health duties. This did not, however, make the borough master in its own house. The county council still had control over the approval of such matters as the town's development plan and proposals for new schools, and was responsible for submitting them to the Government.

As for progress on the promised reforms, the Government bought time by asking local government associations to agree a new system of local government among themselves. It was hardly a serious proposal. Small boroughs were no more likely to vote for their own abolition than county councils would be to surrender large towns of considerable rateable value, such as Poole, which underpinned a county's own finances. It was therefore up to individual authorities to find their own solutions. The proposal from Bournemouth Borough Council was that a joint committee should be formed to consider the amalgamation of Poole and Bournemouth.

As in Victorian times, when Poole declined to opt for county borough status, and surrendered its independence to the county council, there was a case to be made from the standpoint of financial advantage. In the case of amalgamation with Bournemouth, there was the possibility of a more substantial financial gain to Poole, for in 1958, Poole's rate was 19s 1d (95p) in the £, compared with 12s 4d (61.6p) in Bournemouth. But Poole councillors also felt that with so much needing to be done in their borough, in the way of making up and lighting roads, and slum clearance, Bournemouth was sure to demand a differential rate for Poole, just as it did when it took over Winton from the county council.

There were other serious doubts about the proposal for a combined council of 29 Bournemouth representatives and 16 from Poole. These 45 councillors would also elect 15 aldermen, and Poole feared its voice on such a council would be drowned. It already had the example of the county council to cite. Poole contributed more than a third of the county rate but had only 19 county councillors out of 93, and only one county alderman. It could also point to a groundswell of opinion against an earlier proposal from Bournemouth that the boroughs should amalgamate.

Public opinion in Poole regarded such proposals as a take-over rather than a merger, because it feared they could lead to the older borough losing its strong sense of community. Poole had its own mayor, sheriff, recorder, magistrates' court and quarter sessions. The mayor also carried the title of Admiral of the Port of Poole, and was chairman of the Poole Harbour Commissioners, while the council had the right to elect half the members of the board of Commissioners. It was proud of the maritime traditions symbolised by the ancient ceremony of beating the bounds of Poole Harbour. All these rights and privileges might well be swept away, along with more recent civic developments, such as the council-owned water and works departments, the latter then carrying out more than a million pounds' worth of housing and school building contracts.

Bournemouth was not wholly unsympathetic to Poole's misgivings. Its representatives said they understood that Poole had a long and historic past, but although civic tradition had little bearing on modern conditions, it was a valuable asset that it might be possible to preserve and develop in any amalgamation. However, in the last resort, efficiency and economic necessity would have to over-ride the claims of tradition. The response to this from a specially convened meeting of Poole Borough Council was that 'having considered every aspect of amalgamation...and having given consideration to all factors involved, no further action be taken with regard to such an amalgamation.'

In October 1954 another specially convened meeting of the council approved for submission to Parliament a draft Bill to create a county borough of Poole. The intention was that it should take control of all local authority powers, but have a joint police force with Bournemouth and a joint fire service with Dorset County Council. The resolution was carried by 33 votes to nil. Alderman Geoffrey Bravery, and Councillors Leonard Matchan and Ronald Hart, abstained, their motion to defer the proposal having been defeated. The Bill was deposited in Parliament, after public consultation, in November 1954. Shortly afterwards, Dorset County Council resolved by 68 votes to 11 to oppose it. The 68 votes included that of Commander R H Baker, Poole's only county alderman!

Despite earlier public feeling against amalgamation with Bournemouth, not all Poole ratepayers were in favour of seeking county borough status, and some maintained that they did not know what it involved, either for them or for the town. It was now that the distinction drawn by Bournemouth between civic tradition and modern conditions made itself apparent in this context. The Society of Poole Men, which prided itself as a public watchdog and guardian of that tradition, called upon the Sheriff of Poole to hold a public meeting at which the purpose of the Bill could be explained.

The practice of holding Sheriff's Meetings or similar gatherings on important civic issues was an old-established one, and the Sheriff, Bill Cole, a member of an old Poole family, was fiercely proud of the traditions of the town, and of his office in particular. His role in civic life, however, had been somewhat circumscribed by the fact that he had lost his seat as a councillor at the previous municipal elections. Although he had still been elected by the council to the office of Sheriff, he was unable to take part in debates in the council chamber; and this was a subject dear to his heart.

He therefore had an opportunity to regain the public stage by calling such a meeting at the Municipal Buildings on 3rd January 1955. Councillor Arthur

Lloyd-Allen, chairman of the Finance Committee, explained the purpose of the Bill and why it was being promoted. After this rather lengthy speech, the Sheriff invited questions from the meeting. 'Remember, though,' he cried, 'Big Brother at Dorchester is watching you!'

Some of those present were unamused by this characterisation of the county council as a sinister eminence in the background. Irritation soon gave way to outright fury when a further announcement was made which seemed to show that the anticipated debate on the issue would not, after all, be taking place. Those who had come prepared to argue both sides of the case were informed that a formal public meeting had already been held prior to the submission of the Bill, and that the Sheriff's Meeting had been called solely to explain the reasons for promoting it.

This turned the fury back upon Mr Cole. Speakers from the floor protested that it was absurd for the Sheriff to call a meeting, appoint himself as chairman, refuse to take a motion, and stifle all opposition. What right had he to do this? Very little, according to another speaker, who declared that there was no basis in law for a so-called 'Sheriff's Meeting' and that the whole proceedings were a farce. Nothing that the Sheriff, or anyone else on the platform, could say was capable of appeasing the dissidents, and as feelings ran higher, the meeting got out of hand.

Morris Hart, a barrister from Branksome Park, was joined by several others as he gathered his papers and left. 'I've looked into this, and there's no such thing as a Sheriff's Meeting. Never has been!' he cried. In any event, he felt, Poole's case had been put to the meeting with a most undesirable emphasis upon personalities. One of Poole's small band of county councillors, Harvey Banister, later declared that the occasion showed he was wise to vote in favour of objecting to the Bill, because the county council had not been allowed to put its case to the Sheriff's Meeting.

Claims that the meeting's terms of reference prevented the case against county borough status being debated were hotly contested and ridiculed. One of the protestors tore down the public notice from the foyer of the Municipal Buildings and sent it to Donald Gould, editor of the *Poole and Dorset Herald*, who reprinted part it, together with an announcement that the *Herald* would call its own meeting of townsfolk the following Sunday.

The notice of the Sheriff's Meeting stated that it was being held 'with a view to informing local residents of the advantages or otherwise of Poole becoming a county borough.' It was all too clear after the walk-out that local residents had wanted to have their say, not merely to be informed and to have their questions answered. Those left behind were completely nonplussed. Eventually it was lamely agreed to adjourn the Sheriff's Meeting for a week. The question of whether Mr Cole had any right as Sheriff to call it in the first place was brushed aside by subsequent events.

Nevertheless, it was undoubtedly the case that there had been scores of Sheriff's Meetings in Poole over the centuries. Before the Municipal Corporations Act, 1835, when the town was governed by fifty or sixty self-elected Burgesses, it was a custom that if any ten of them disagreed with a decision of the Corporation, they had the right to call on the Sheriff for such a meeting, at which the public could air its views. While it was true that no Act of Parliament ever enshrined this practice, none had ever abolished it, and in Poole, the tradition was older than Parliament itself. The last Sheriff's Meeting had been called a few years previously when Alderman Bravery was Sheriff. But on 3rd January 1955, Alderman Bravery was among the objectors to county borough status and to the conduct and status of the meeting itself, who stormed out into the night!

It was also due to Alderman Bravery that the *Herald* was able to announce its plan for an alternative public meeting. It took place in the Regent Theatre, a cinema in High Street, of which he was the proprietor. Donald Gould took the chair and imposed himself firmly upon the conduct of the meeting, with the aid of a set of traffic lights installed on the stage. Speakers had to start their address on the green light, and finish as soon as the signal turned to red. But this time there would be no impediments to putting both sides of the argument.

It proved to be a lively occasion, attended by some seven hundred and fifty people. Councillor Lloyd-Allen began with a detailed explanation of the reasons for promoting the Bill, and Morris Hart led the opposition. Gradually, however, it became clear that the vast majority of those present supported the effort to gain county borough status. After a rousing speech from Miss Audrey Kaye, of Canford Cliffs Young Conservatives, the question was put. The show of hands was overwhelmingly in favour of the Bill.

Fervid local support counted for little at Westminster. On the second reading of the Bill, Duncan Sandys, Minister of Housing and Local Government, intervened to say that the Government did not support it, and would not support any such Bills before its own legislation to reform the system had been introduced. The Government was, however, stung into some sort of action a few months later, when it announced a proposal to set up another Parliamentary Commission.

The Local Government Act 1958 created separate Commissions for England and Wales to review the boundaries and status of local authorities. The Commissioners would be able to recommend the creation of county boroughs with less than 100,000 population, provided there were special circumstances. Poole's case was urged during a debate on the legislation by its Member of Parliament, Captain Richard Pilkington.

He told the House that Poole did not rely on population alone to get a speedy implementation of its proposals for county borough status. There were other factors which the Commission might wish to take into account, such as its situation in relation to the rest of Dorset.

Poole was in one corner of the county, said Captain Pilkington, who went on to praise 'its history, which is long and distinguished; its efficiency, which is outstanding; its reputation, which is excellent; its individuality, which is pronounced; and finally, its patience, which it has shared with other boroughs which have waited a long time. I hope the Minister will once again give a decided and decisive reassurance on this matter.'

He was assured that the Commission would get to work as quickly as possible, once it was set up, but that whether Poole would be at the very top of the list was a matter for the Commissioners. They would consider the fitness of a proposed county borough to discharge its functions, the viability of the county without the new county borough; and would assume that a population of 100,000 was large enough for county borough status.

The council prepared its case after consultations with the Member of Parliament, but in 1962, it was still patiently awaiting a visit from the Commissioners.

*'The Town Hall, the nursery of democracy, should not be allowed to become a mere reminder of local government. The essential feature of local government is that it is local. Our system has now been so denuded of functions that its very existence is in danger...Unless people take a keen interest in the government of its local affairs, the Town Hall will come to house only civil servants, instructed by remote control, immune from local protests and opinion, wrapped in a cloak of some Whitehall office.'*

*Wilson Kenyon, Town Clerk of Poole, 1955.*

# Development of the Old Town

The authors of the plan to bring a new life and sense of purpose to the decaying heart of the Old Town were in no doubt about the problem: it no longer functioned as Poole's central area. Nor did it epitomise the character and personality of a great and expanding borough.

Even the hundreds of ancient buildings, a legacy of the stagnation which had befallen parts of the Old Town, constituted a mixed blessing. Many dated from the 18th century days of the prosperous Newfoundland trade. The borough council had a list of more than 500 dwellings which it considered should be removed, because the Medical Officer of Health reported that they were a danger to health and incapable of being made fit for human occupation. Of these, more than 100 were listed as of architectural or historic interest.

Not only had ancient houses survived, because of a lack of economic impetus for change. Apart from the addition of West Quay Road and Green Road, the width and pattern of many of the roads in the Old Town were literally medieval. The juxtaposition in narrow streets of homes and industry, however, did not mean they were integrated into a community in which people both lived and worked. The population of the 176.7 acres of the Old Town development area in 1958 was approximately 4,665, almost exactly the same as in 1801 at the height of the Newfoundland trade. About 4,600 people, approximately one-sixth of Poole's working population, had jobs in the Old Town; but of these, probably less than 10% also lived there.

How had the Old Town become fixed in its present unattractive pattern? The planners explained that between 1875 and 1914 its Georgian buildings were almost completely encircled by a belt of warehouses and factories, including a greatly expanded gasworks, and the space between was filled with artisans' dwellings.

The Town Map, outlining the future development of Poole, had been submitted to the Minister of Housing and Local Government in 1952, and was approved by him in 1954: but it contained no proposals for comprehensive redevelopment of the Old Town, merely stating that a further plan would be prepared to deal with it.

The area presented many complex and unique problems. Achieving the objectives of such a plan would be more difficult than identifying them. The first objective was to eliminate the level crossings in High Street and Towngate Street; eliminate through traffic from High Street, and replace the obsolete road pattern; and to provide adequate car parks. The second was to ensure appropriate redevelopment of areas of slum and outworn property. The third objective was to retain the more important of the buildings which had been listed as of special architectural or historic interest, without seriously prejudicing the proper redevelopment of the area as a whole. Lastly, it was important that the redevelopment proposals were an economic possibility, and that they did not cause undue dislocation while the plan was being implemented.

The most satisfactory way to eliminate the bottle-necks of the level crossing and Poole Bridge would be a high-level diversion of the railway north-east of the Old Town, and a high-level bridge over the harbour. But on investigation, these proved to be only remote possibilities, because of their high cost and low priority in a national context, so there was no justification for including them in a development plan. The only practicable alternative was to plan a new road which bridged the railway. It was decided this should be sited near the railway station, as having considerably less effect on existing properties than attempting to raise existing roads over the railway.

A lateral 'traffic way' was then proposed, which would connect the new road to be built over the railway with Poole Bridge. This new road would relieve High Street of all through traffic. It had been estimated that some 40% of traffic in the Old Town was on its way to, or from, Hamworthy. The traffic way would overcome serious congestion in High Street, allow it to function purely as a shopping street, and avoid the need to widen the street, thus leaving valuable shop property undisturbed. The new road would also relieve West Quay Road and allow it to function as the main service road for its substantial industries.

But there was still the baffling problem of how to provide Poole with adequate shopping facilities. High Street had been the main shopping centre for very many years: but for a population then approaching 90,000, and expected to grow by around 1,000 a year, it constituted little more than what would have been regarded as a secondary shopping area in other towns of that size. Much of the local population's spending power was supporting the economy of Bournemouth through the wide range of shops and goods available beyond County Gates. The 1950 Census of Distribution of Retail Trade showed that an average of £104.7 for each resident of Poole was spent in Poole shops, but the comparative figures for other towns were: Bournemouth, £236, Weymouth, £157.9, Wimborne, £258.6 and Blandford £350.6. A later report by the Town Clerk drew a comparison with Burnley, Rochdale, Rotherham, and Darlington, four northern industrial towns of similar size to Poole, with no particularly favourable trading conditions. It estimated that for Poole's retail trade to equal the average of these towns, it would have to achieve increases ranging from 200% for furniture to 20% for grocery.

The first thought of the planners was to extend shopping facilities south of the level crossings, but this proved impossible. North of the railway line, in the Longfleet area, some shops had been established by building out into the gardens of old villas on the western side of High Street, and others had been built on the opposite side. The idea of developing Ladies' Walking Field for shopping came as a shock. During a visit to County Hall, Dorchester, the Town Clerk was suddenly asked, by an assistant town planning officer of Dorset County Council, if he thought the borough council could be persuaded to agree to it. The Town Clerk did not commit himself, but agreed to put the proposition to Alderman Lloyd-Allen, chairman of the Finance Committee. *'I don't know',*' replied the Alderman, *'but if you can convince me, I'll convince the council!'*

Such a revolutionary proposal was not likely to receive the immediate approval of the council, let alone the traders of High Street, or the owners and occupiers of neighbouring properties that would have to be acquired. Furthermore, Ladies' Walking Field was legally a public open space, and therefore subject to special protection unless it was replaced elsewhere. As well as its recreational and community uses, there were vague plans by the Committee for Education to use it for extending or rebuilding Poole Grammar School.

Although the planners' objectives may have been laudable, and indeed public-spirited, it was obvious from the state of the Old Town that change, progress, slum clearance, redevelopment and road improvement were not familiar concepts to those who lived and worked there. The issues therefore became simplified in the public mind: families would be forced to leave; historic buildings would be pulled down to build an unnecessary new road between Hunger Hill and Poole Bridge; and Ladies' Walking Field would be lost to new shopping. This in turn would compete unfairly with established businesses south of the level crossings. Yet one of the crossings, and the gasworks, would remain as they were for the time being.

These fears, plus the very real fears of the high cost of implementing the proposals, and of the possible failure of the proposed new shopping area, were reflected in the minds of many members of the borough council. An additional moral factor was brought into the debate by Jack Valentine, the president of the Society of Poole Men, who alleged that Ladies' Walking Field had been given to the town by Lady Wimborne to be used as a public open space for ever. It was a canard that became part of local legend and was never allowed to be finally laid to rest.

Even the title had come to acquire a misplaced emotive significance in some minds. Few ladies of the town would have chosen to walk on this nondescript grassy area, often waterlogged, and overlooked by a gasworks, railway line, bus station and car park, when they could enjoy the delights of Poole Park a few hundred yards away. It was a long piece of ground on which ropes were once twisted by women employees of the Longfleet Rope Works. Often coveted by the old Corporations, it was not acquired until the early nineteen-hundreds. Lord Wimborne wanted the Corporation's unused waterworks land at Lilliput to add to his brother's Parkstone Golf Course, and an exchange was agreed, with both pieces of land being valued at £6,000. It was used as a recreation ground by boys of the adjoining Poole Grammar School, as well as for circuses and the annual Poole Flower Show. People became fond of this rough field, which accounted for a substantial part of the open space in the Old Town plan area.

Confined to east and west by the waters of Parkstone Bay and Holes Bay, and by two level crossings to the north, the Old Town was already choking to death in 1950. Most of the houses had been poorly built in the first place. Many had been run up quickly in the early eighteen-hundreds to accommodate a surge in population during and just after the Napoleonic wars. Properties had been neglected for decades; many of even the smaller ones were divided into multiple occupation. Larger ones, abandoned by their owners, had been taken over by vagrants. At first sight, the fact that most were long past any hope of repair might have been expected to facilitate a wholesale reconstruction of the Old Town, for there should have been little opposition to their clearance. But it was not as simple as that. In the early nineteen-fifties, the Royal Commission on Historical Monuments recommended the listing of 328 buildings as being of architectural or historic interest. After an appeal by the borough council, the

*Gentleman asleep in Ladies' Walking Field opposite what is today Poole Arts Centre.*

buildings were examined by the chief architect of the Commission, and in 1954 the Ministry agreed that 131 should be listed as of special interest, and a further 140 placed on a supplemental list of buildings which, it was hoped, could be preserved.

The planners' solution to this problem was to form what they first called a 'garden precinct' in an area roughly between Thames Street, the traffic way, High Street and Market Place. It would, they argued, be a much more valuable way of preserving the more important of the listed buildings, than trying to preserve isolated buildings, which would become incongruous in redeveloped surroundings. The precinct would preserve ancient buildings in their original street setting. Non-conforming uses, and properties incapable of restoration, would be replaced with houses to match existing ones. This proposal for what is now officially described as a Conservation Area must have been a precursor of many other similar schemes.

*23 and 24 Skinner Street one of the better preserved old houses of the Old Town, originally built in 1786 as a single house but it had, like many of the Old Poole houses, been partly rebuilt and divided into two houses in 1833.*

## *THE PROPOSED PRECINCT AREA*

It was decided that it was impossible to retrieve some twenty domestic properties in the area of the proposed precinct and these were included in slum clearance orders, leaving other properties which did not conform with the establishment of a precinct to be dealt with later.

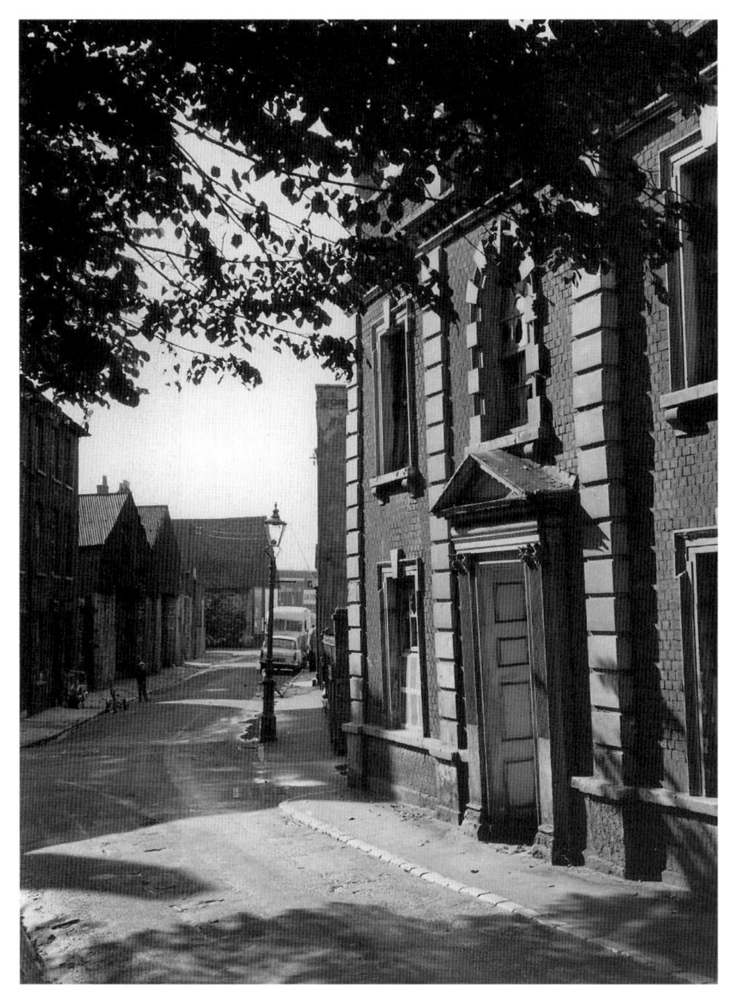

*Thames Street, looking towards the Quay. Warehouses and public lavatories were on the left hand side and Poole House was structurally unsound prior to its conversion into showers and changing rooms for workers at the ironfoundry which lay immediately behind it. Just beyond Poole House was the Mansion House, then used as a lodging house mainly by long-distance lorry drivers.*

*Looking up Church Street from the Mansion House in Thames Street.*

*West Street ran northwards from Thames Street along the west side of St.James Church.*

*Church Street. Some old timber-framed houses had been demolished some years earlier and a scrap yard had been formed on the site. Blenheim House, on the corner of Cinnamon Lane was owned by the Corporation to house a member of the Parks staff.*

*Looking south down Church Street from the corner of Levets Lane, towards St. James's Church.*

*(Above) On the corner of New Street and Market Street, 1960.*

*(Right) New Street looking towards Market Street, with Cinnamon Lane entering from the left, past the large derelict ostlery. On the right was the mansion of the Whites, old Poole merchants. It was derelict in 1960 with its roof collapsed. Nos. 6 and 8 New Street were the only mansions of old Poole incapable of restoration.*

*Market Street, near the Guildhall, 1962.*

*The old Greyhound Inn on the corner of King Street at the side of the Guildhall. Built 1770 but had later been divided into two shops.*

Survey and planning work for the redevelopment proposals commenced in 1952, but it was not until 1957 that a draft plan was arrived at that was suitable for wider public consultation. The planners knew they would have to explain how all other options had been carefully investigated before proposing so much demolition and redevelopment. They arranged to put their case to a special meeting of the Redevelopment Committee early in 1957. But before they could do so - indeed, before most members of the council knew anything about the matter - their proposals were leaked to the *Poole and Dorset Herald*, which highlighted them in stark detail.

*Far-sighted townsmen saw the end of Poole...Business below the level crossing will wane and die...Will sabotage the plan for enlarging Poole Grammar School...* the paper declared, before going on to report the council's positive aims, which included compensating for the loss of Ladies' Walking Field by reclaiming extra land for open space at Baiter. Thus the proposals for Baiter, which in 1960 would be considered at the same public inquiry as the comprehensive redevelopment map for the Old Town, became embroiled in the Ladies' Walking Field saga.

Passions were only cooled by the suggestion that further consideration of the plan should be deferred for six months, but this did nothing to abate these early objections. It took some time for a majority of the members of the council even to agree that the plan should be put on public deposit, so that all ratepayers knew what was being proposed and had a chance to comment upon it. Meanwhile, the *Herald* continued to report reaction to what had been leaked: *The town will fight field grab...There are plenty of shops and too few open spaces...* The least emotional comment came from a ratepayer who was reported to have declared: *'There's one consolation. I doubt if they'll ever get round to doing anything!'*

After the public consultation period, the council arranged a public meeting at which the plan could be explained and comments invited. A very crowded meeting at the Municipal Buildings was dominated by those who objected to development of Ladies' Walking Field, and to the demotion of High Street as a through road by the proposed traffic way. Alderman Arthur Butler led the assault. He claimed that the plan 'read like the product of a diseased mind' and would be a disastrous failure that would cost the public dear. Alderman Bill Cole saw no contradiction in asserting that it would force many traders out of business. 'Poole shoppers clapped and cheered,' according to the *Herald.* Not a voice was heard in support of the plan.

After such apparently unanimous opposition, it was, perhaps, unlikely that the council would approve the plan at its subsequent meeting. Alderman Lloyd-Allen proposed that as neither the council members and officers, nor traders and the public, could claim to be experts on the subject, before the plan was considered further, independent consultants should be asked to report on its basic premises: whether there was a need for extra shopping facilities, and if so, where they could be provided. It was a suggestion eagerly seized by the plan's beleaguered supporters, and the motion was approved.

The report commissioned from Goddard and Smith, a London firm of surveyors, valuers and shopping consultants, confirmed the view of the planners that Poole needed more shopping, and that it could not be provided south of the railway with any hope of commercial success. Only then were the consultants asked to report on how best the increased shopping area could be provided. Their report, received in 1958, recommended the extension of Kingland Crescent to join Kingland Road, to enter High Street North at Burdens' Store, with new shops on each side of the extended road, and a new bus station; and using the bulk of Ladies' Walking Field as a car park.

The county planning officer was concerned that such a junction would be dangerous. It would be too close to an enlarged roundabout opposite the George Hotel, needed to serve the proposed bridge over the railway, yet it would be incapable of being incorporated into it. The consultants, however, replied that taking Kingland Crescent into High Street at point nearer to the

Kingland Road, at its junction with High Street.

High Street North in Longfleet. Longfleet Place ran between Burdens' grocery store and Hartnells (formerly Snooks'), the stationers in High Street. Kingland Road enters at the side of Burdens' store.

*(Above) To the side of Belvedere was a warehouse facing Longfleet Place.*
*(Below) To the left of the property shown in the top of page 92 were 'Seacroft and Belvedere', originally the homes of the Burdens whose shop was on the corner of High Street and Kingland Crescent.*

roundabout would entail purchasing so many more properties that the scheme might well prove unprofitable.

The supporters of the original plan were disappointed at these limited proposals for extra shopping, but they were adopted as part of the development plan for submission to the Minister for approval. Members of the council with financial interests in property or businesses in the Old Town, however, were not the only ones still opposed to it. The Highways Committee had for many years been in favour of substantial widening of High Street, an order having been made at one stage to provide a width of 60 feet. Because of the improvement line already declared for High Street, the front portion of three stores, including Woolworths' new store, on the site of the Amity Cinema, had been restricted to a single storey. Now there were fears that traffic might be banned from a street which had served the town for so long, and that new shops north of the railway would have an unfair advantage.

Differences of opinion within the council over the relative merits of a traffic way, against the widening of West Quay Road and High Street, were among the factors which delayed submission of the redevelopment plan. Meanwhile, slum clearance and the building of new council flats had already started in areas of the Old Town where this would not conflict with the plan's proposals. This led to allegations of 'piecemeal planning' and complaints that the council was going ahead with redevelopment before the plan had been made available for public comment.

There were seven members of the council whose financial interests in the Old Town might be affected by the plan. They were warned that they were not allowed to vote, or to take part in any discussion, when the council eventually debated a recommendation to accept it.

'It's a lot of rot!' exploded Alderman Bright. 'What's the point of staying? I have been in High Street 30 years, and on the council 28, and now I cannot speak!'

Alderman Cole, whose family owned a furnishing and undertaking business in High Street, declared: 'There are a number of aldermen and councillors who will go to any lengths to salve their consciences, so that they can justify their action in taking away the people's rights and liberties by taking away the amenities of Ladies' Walking Field. Why,' he added, 'a lot of people in this chamber don't even know where High Street is!'

Alderman Bravery, whose company owned the Regent Theatre in High Street, was asked if he had an interest in the matter. 'Yes - a very direct interest in the welfare of every individual in the borough!' he cried.

After a very emotional debate, the Redevelopment Committee's recommendation to approve the draft development plan, proposed by Alderman Lloyd-Allen, and seconded by Alderman Reeves, was narrowly approved: but only because members with a pecuniary interest had been obliged to abstain from voting.

'We are taking,' said Alderman Lloyd-Allen, 'the first step which can decide the destiny of the borough, not a small section of it. We are planning for the Poole of the future and for the next hundred years. Everyone will have a chance to comment on it, for it will be the subject of a public inquiry after the plan has been on public inspection for ten weeks.'

The issue of increased shopping facilities overshadowed all others during the consultation period, which began in April 1960. Traders did all they could to stimulate further public objections to the plan. Poole Chamber of Trade was unconvinced by the county planning officer's arguments that it was a wonderful opportunity to recover lost trade, and that if Poole did nothing, the deterioration at the bottom of High Street would go on spreading northwards. In July that year, Alderman Cole, now the Mayor, found his own unique way to raise public opposition.

He had been invited by Bertram Mills' Circus to open its first night in the 'big top' on Ladies' Walking Field. The ringmaster led him to the centre of the ring. 'Do you like having circuses on Ladies' Walking Field?' the Mayor asked. There was an immediate shrill response from hundreds of children and parents. As the cheering died down, Alderman Cole pointed to the Town Clerk, who was also in the audience, and said: 'He wants to put shops and a car park here! You don't - do you?' This time, there was a shrill cry of 'No!' 'Never mind,' the Mayor called back, 'It'll never happen!'

Some members of the council were becoming restive. In August, thirteen of them put down a motion *that the Kingland Crescent development be not proceeded with and that the areas off the High Street below the Level Crossing be planned for an expansion of the existing shopping area.* At the September meeting, Alderman Butler again led the attack. Determined not to be silenced by allegations of pecuniary interest, he announced: 'I have sold my shareholding in Debenhams, who have a drapery store in High Street, and I now have no financial interest in any shop in Poole, or within 25 miles of Poole.'

During another emotional debate, he rounded on 'sleeping beauties' who still insisted that trade was moving north toward Longfleet. 'The firms who know would never be persuaded to take sites north of the level crossing,' he declared. 'Clever salesmen will be used, with the sanction of this council, to persuade traders and others, who may not know the true facts, to take shops in Kingland Crescent, where, for many, there will be no hope of ever establishing a profitable business.' The motion was defeated by 15 votes to 10 after Alderman Cole, and five other council members, declared interests which prevented them taking part or voting in the debate.

Alderman Butler resumed his barrage of criticism at the public inquiry into the plan which was held in November 1960, tabling a 32-page proof of evidence, plus more than a dozen appendices, in support of his contention that the plan would be financially bad for ratepayers and injurious to Poole's shopping amenities. For seven days, every aspect of the plan was questioned by individual objectors, as well as representatives of traders, the Society of Poole Men, and other organisations. Alderman Butler based his remarks on some thirty years' experience of department store retailing in Bournemouth and Poole: the residents of Love Lane, which stood in the path of the traffic way, spoke as members of a close-knit community which did not wish to be uprooted. 'No amount of compensation would make up for the loss of my home, which I bought with my life's savings,' said one man, aged 72.

After so much hostility to the plan over the preceding months, it was understandable that its advocates would seek the occasion to redress the balance during the inquiry. *'Everyone, from bank managers to station masters, has apparently purchased a do-it-yourself kit and feels himself qualified to solve the problems of the Old Town,'* said Mr John Pryer, summing up for the planning authority, after twenty-seven objectors had put their case. He claimed that, having regard to the number of persons represented at the inquiry, the interest shown by the inhabitants of the Old Town itself had been 'pathetic.'

It was not until January 1963 that the Minister announced his approval of the plan's proposals for the area south of the railway; the new roads, including the traffic way, the Hunger Hill roundabout, and a bridge over the railway; and the establishment of a special precinct of historic buildings. He also approved the principle of providing new shops north of the railway, but not the proposed layout and distribution of shops. A possible solution, he suggested, was to extend Kingland Crescent to a point in High Street nearer to the George Hotel.

Meanwhile, the resolve of council members supporting the development plan had been severely tested. For three years, by strict economies in running expenses, and using profits made by its works department and water undertaking, the council had held its rate steady: but in 1962, the dam burst. The county council precept rose by nearly two shillings (10p) in the £, to which cuts in Government grants added more than 6d (2.5p): and with the council's own increased costs, the borough rate had to be raised by a record four shillings (20p) in the £. This led to strong protests by all the town's ratepayers' associations. Alderman Herbert Ballam contrasted the weight of local taxation in Poole with that in Bournemouth and claimed the council was doing too much, too soon, and should slow down.

The council's officers were made aware of the Minister's thoughts on the shopping issue before his official decision was announced. Geoffrey Hopkinson had been appointed to the newly created post of Borough Architect and Planning Officer in July 1960, and Robert Hawker succeeded to the post of

Borough Engineer in 1963. Together they played the major part in preparing a new plan on the lines suggested by the Minister, to include a roundabout at the George Hotel that could also serve a bridge over the railway, when that was built. Within the large area between a realigned Kingland Road and the railway line, they designed a traffic-free shopping precinct.

The Redevelopment Committee proceeded cautiously. It appointed new consultants, Hillier, Parker, May and Rowden, to advise them on the feasibility of new shopping facilities south of the railway. In September 1962 the consultants reported that 'additional shopping space leading off High Street below the level crossings...would be neither practicable nor desirable, though existing owners should be encouraged to increase the amount of shopping by individual development.'

The following month the council decided to ask the consultants for a further report on developing the area north of the railway, with Kingland Road extended to join the George roundabout, along the lines of the officers' new plan. This report was received in December 1962. The consultants were of the opinion that it would be a viable proposition to build a pedestrian shopping precinct, even though 26 business premises and 29 small houses would have to be acquired and demolished.

*Plan showing the proposed realignment of Kingland Road, the 'George' roundabout and the bridge over the railway.*

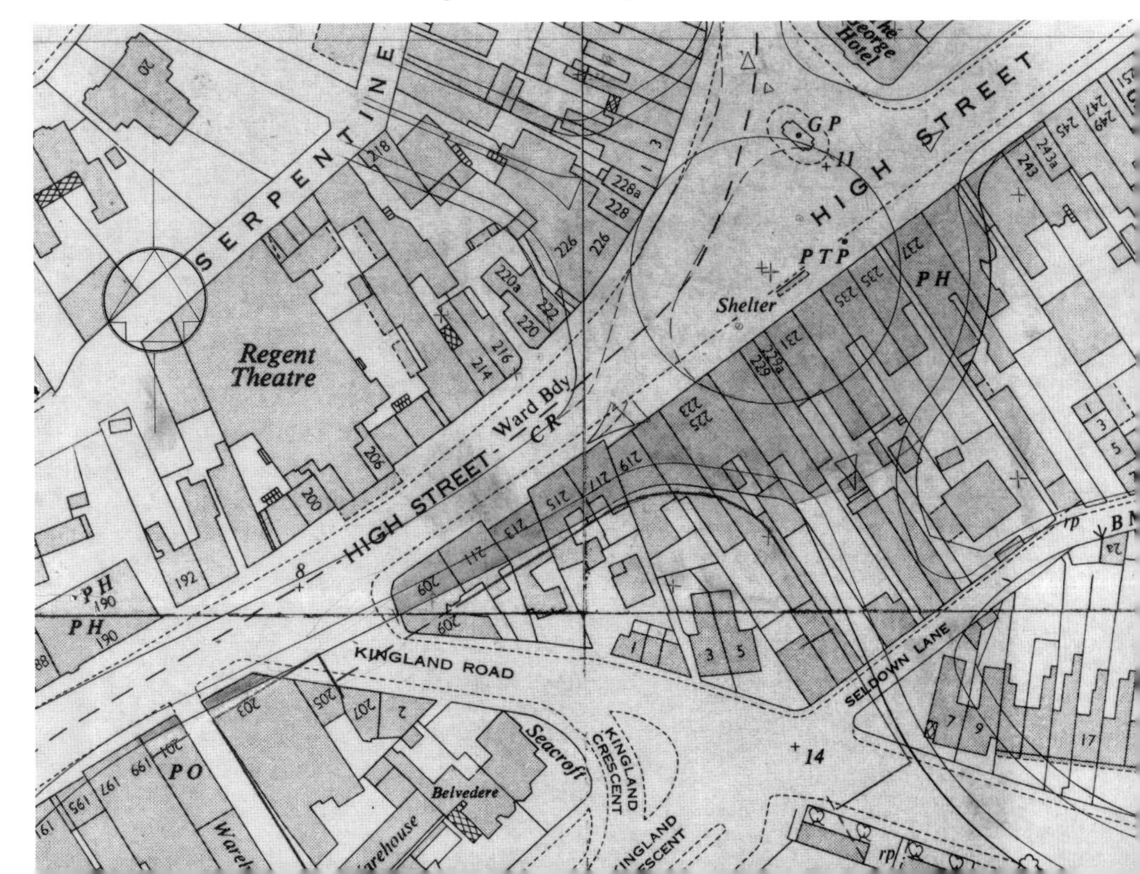

The committee accepted the report, and its recommendation to adopt it was approved at a special evening meeting of the council in January 1963. Opposition to the scheme continued to the last, with the Member of Parliament siding with objectors to the loss of Ladies' Walking Field, and High Street traders obtaining a contrary report from their own consultants, which endorsed their view that only a modest increase in shopping was required, and that this could be provided south of the railway.

In September 1960, Alderman Butler had warned the council against 'clever salesmen' being used to sell 'dud propositions.' By March 1963, less than a fortnight after the first advertisements appeared, the council had received more than 120 inquiries from developers and others interested in the scheme to provide nearly 60 shops in a traffic-free precinct. The argument over the future of trade in the Old Town was at last about to be settled, once and for all.

*'It's time the High Street tail stopped wagging the Poole dog.'*

*Alderman Reeves, 1960.*

*'I weep when I remember how I used to gambol in inch-deep mud,'*

*Terry Coleman in an article on Ladies' Walking Field in Poole Herald, 1960.*

*'The new 'traffic way' was aligned to disturb as few of the listed buildings as possible, but two which were 100-200 years old and six of over 80 years would have to be demolished.'*

*Report to Council, September 1961.*

# The Baiter Reclamation

The draft Poole Town Map of 1952 originally proposed the reclamation of 82 acres of mudland from Parkstone Bay for development as public open space. This area was reduced to 26.5 acres, after strong opposition from Parkstone Yacht Club and residents of Whitecliff and the Elms Estate, but the proposal went to a public inquiry after the council refused to give the Parkstone Bay Protection Society an undertaking never to propose any further reclamation in the bay. The Minister approved the 26.5 acre scheme in November 1954.

In 1957, when the use of Ladies' Walking Field for shops, a bus station, and car park was being considered, the council opened negotiations to purchase the mudlands needed for this scheme, and obtained planning permission from Dorset County Council. The following year, a scheme to reclaim 43 acres was produced, which sought to reduce the cost of building the sea wall, by taking a shorter, more direct line between Baiter and Whitecliff. At the same time, it would enable more land to be reclaimed for

*Part of the area which was reclaimed at Baiter, with Poole Gasworks in the background.*

open space, for the relatively small cost of the extra filling material required, which would compensate for loss of Ladies' Walking Field.

This scheme also included a second tunnel under the railway embankment in Whitecliff Road; a pedestrian footbridge over the railway from Park Lake Road; public conveniences, a cafe, and beach chalets, as well as a new slipway and fishermen's hard, adjoining Fishermen's Dock, and sites for six blocks of flats adjoining the gasworks site, the last-named intended to help finance the £401,000 estimated cost.

The council's planning application was called in by the Minister as a major departure from the development plan approved in 1957, and was the subject of a public inquiry immediately following the inquiry into the Old Town redevelopment plan. It was opposed by the Dorset Lake Association and 37 residents. There were also differences between the borough council and Dorset County Council over the inclusion of flats and the status of a proposed road between Baiter and Whitecliff. The county wanted it to be a 'marine drive' with a speed limit and restrictions on commercial traffic similar to those in Poole Park.

The borough council had already decided in July 1960 to go ahead with reclaiming an area lying to the west of the Baiter peninsula, which was covered by the 1957 planning permission, using hardcore from slum clearance demolition sites in the Old Town, but mainly overburden from the Royal Doulton claypit at Hamworthy and the South Western Pottery at Parkstone.

*Reclamation in progress between Baiter and Whitecliff.*

The Minister's decision to grant outline permission for the 43-acre scheme was announced in June 1961. He said it should form 'an attractive area of open space, and be particularly useful for residents in the town centre.' Although it would affect the foreground of the view enjoyed by Whitecliff residents, this would be a comparatively minor intrusion, of no significance compared to the public amenities that would result.

Permission was also granted to erect not more than 100 flats, in blocks no taller than five storeys, but the Minister declined to impose a speed limit or traffic restrictions on the new road. His decision marked the start of a public controversy over the road scheme that would continue for the next three decades, until it was finally abandoned by the borough council.

Such generous provision of new open space should have satisfied the defenders of Ladies' Walking Field, but their vigilance remained undimmed when it was announced in December 1963 that reclamation work at Baiter had stopped until the spring, and that sports pitches would not be available there until the following autumn. A short list of four companies to compete for the shopping centre contract had already been drawn up, and there were angry protests that the council had been promised that work would not start on Ladies' Walking Field before Baiter was ready.

'I deny the fact of an actual pledge,' said Geoffrey Adams, chairman of the Redevelopment Committee, 'but there has been confident hope that one would be ready before the other is taken.

*Ladies' Walking Field prior to redevelopment.*

# Sewerage

The high reputation and 'clean beach' awards enjoyed today by the miles of sandy shore eastwards from Sandbanks owe a good deal to efforts which began in 1953 to end the discharge of sewage into Poole Bay from nine separate outfalls - two in Poole, six in Bournemouth, and one in Christchurch.

In the early post-war years Poole Borough Council had relied on reviving the tentative pre-war agreement between the boroughs of Poole, Bournemouth and Christchurch to have a joint scheme which dealt with the sewage of the three towns. Poole felt that such a scheme would deal with the bulk of its sewerage problems. It was also planned to erect a new sewage works at Hamworthy, which would deal with the whole of that area and, with the agreement with Wareham and Purbeck Rural Council, the sewage of Upton. Poole's Medical Officer of Health was concerned that the existing works at Hamworthy were a potential risk to health. Sewage was taken to a small, old plant on the southern shore of Holes Bay, into which the filtered effluent was drained. In the northern part of Poole it had been agreed that the drainage of Merley would be dealt with by the councils of Wimborne as part of their proposed sewerage scheme.

The situation in Poole was more acute than in Bournemouth and Christchurch. Poole's population was increasing rapidly, and despite some sewer extensions, as late as 1960 there were still 818 cesspools and 185 pail closets in use in Poole. The Broadstone and Hamworthy sewage works had become grossly overloaded by 1953. In the very wettest weather, the Broadstone works became so flooded that they were rendered completely inoperative.

With the lack of any progress on the joint drainage committee's consultations, Poole had decided in 1951 that, whatever the final arrangements were for a joint scheme, the Broadstone works had to be rebuilt, if only to cope with the drainage of the Waterloo Estate, which it was then building. When Wareham and Purbeck Council withdrew from the agreement for the new Hamworthy works to deal with the sewage of Upton, Poole decided to divert Hamworthy drainage to the proposed new works at Broadstone, at a cost of £98,270, rather than to erect works at Hamworthy.

Following a public inquiry into the scheme, the council had applied in 1951 for Government approval to borrow the necessary money for the Broadstone works. Unfortunately, the Government's recurring financial problems meant that approval was delayed, and it was only when the Member of Parliament raised the matter in the Commons that the borough received a reply. This, however, was only to state that approval would have to wait until the next financial year, and that it would write to the council again after April 1953.

Loan sanction was received in 1953 and the work was put in hand that year. Poole had long considered that the most economical means of diverting sewage from sea outfalls would be one single large-scale scheme. In 1955, as work on the first rebuilding of the Broadstone works was being completed, the council decided to go ahead with its own scheme for diverting sewage from the Bay to an enlarged works at Broadstone, and applied for permission to borrow £186,000 for the work. Poole's Medical Officer of Health could see that discharges into the Bay would not be eliminated for some time, but his immediate concern was the urgent need to reduce the load on the sewers between Park Gates East and the outfall at Shore Road, Sandbanks, which discharged sewage from a population of 33,000. The council agreed that sewage from the Old Town, and south-western areas of Poole, should be diverted to Broadstone, which would reduce the discharge at Shore Road to a population of 16,000.

*The Broadstone Sewage Works after its reconstruction and enlargement, 1961.*

The Minister had meanwhile ordered a public inquiry into the application for further extensions at Broadstone in January 1956. While impressed with the council's proposals, he warned that final approval would be given only in stages, because of Government restrictions on capital spending. The council's hopes of early approval were dashed that autumn, when the Chancellor of the Exchequer wrote to every local authority demanding an immediate review of capital expenditure. The need to economise and ensure national stability was such that even works already authorised were not to be undertaken unless urgently needed.

These restrictions put an end to the council's plans for completing a new sewerage system for Poole in four years. The scheme for re-sewering the Old Town and south-western areas was only the first stage. The second, submitted for Ministry approval in 1960, was to divert sewage from Oakdale and Tatnam to the new works, and the third would deal with Branksome, Upper Parkstone, Penn Hill, and Branksome Park. In the final stage, a separate works would be built on land to be acquired from Dorset County Council, which would deal with the rest of Lower Parkstone, Lilliput and Sandbanks, when sea outfalls could be dispensed with.

By 1957, work was well advanced on diverting sewage from the Old Town, which involved extensive road closures over the Christmas and New Year period, as well as thrust boring under the main railway line. By 1960 the Broadstone works would have expanded over the nine and a half acres of its existing site. Another 19 acres of land at Planefield House would be needed for further extensions to deal with a total population of 130,000. Other projects included a £71,000 pumping station for East Quay and an additional diversion scheme for Hamworthy (£98,000).

The first stage of the Oakdale diversion involved laying a new sewer from Fleetsbridge to the Shah of Persia junction. In Fernside Road, there were so many pipes and cables to contend with that it had to be laid in the centre of the highway, which in turn meant closing the road to all traffic. Another length of sewer, from Jolliffe Road to the New Inn, was laid in a deep tunnel so that the roads along its route could remain open.

Poole was proud of its position as the first of the three boroughs to start work on cleaning-up the Bay. Yet to those who may have been less committed, the value of these achievements was somewhat undercut by a report from the Medical Research Council on sewage on bathing beaches, which in 1959 asserted: *'Except where the concentration of sewage is such as to be aesthetically revolting, the risk to health of bathing in sewage contaminated sea water can, for all practical purposes, be ignored.'* To critics of the council's capital spending it could well have seemed a considerable outlay to achieve what might after all amount to no more than an aesthetic improvement. But such a view could scarcely seem less complacent now than the suggestion that sewage in sea water was a problem only when it was visible.

# The Poole Waterworks

Poole Corporation had been responsible for the supply of water since 1910, when it responded to public pressure and bought out the Poole Waterworks Company, which had never been able to provide a constant and satisfactory supply.

After the second world war, demand for water rose sharply, and the Corporation developed a new supply at Sturminster Marshall, where it built a pumping station. During 1952 the demand for water reached 1,502 million gallons, but the borough council was always concerned to ensure the purity of the supply. At least ten samples a month were taken from consumers' taps by sanitary inspectors and submitted for bacteriological examination to the public health laboratory. There was also regular testing of samples in the water undertaking's own laboratory, the results of which were reported to the council every month.

The council was proud of its undertaking. By the nineteen-fifties most of its capital debt in establishing the works had been repaid, and it considered the water rate demanded from its customers of 1s 7d (8p) in the £ was modest. It was therefore with some reluctance that it complied with the Government's request to extend its area of supply to nearby rural areas, for further capital would have to be expended, in return for little income from low-rated rural properties. In 1956 it took over responsibility for the supply of tap water to Shapwick, Sturminster Marshall and Lytchett Matravers, but this modest extension did not satisfy the Government. It urged the borough council to extend into the rest of the county and suggested that Dorset County Council should prepare a scheme for the whole of its own area, the greater part of which still had no piped water supply. Even when Poole was included, it was stated, only 68 per cent of Dorset residents had water on tap, and the Government threatened compulsory action to extend the supply.

Poole Borough Council called a conference of all boroughs, urban and rural districts in east Dorset for exploratory talks on extending its area of supply. There were a number of meetings of representatives from Blandford, Wareham, Swanage, and Sturminster Newton before agreement was reached, but it was at the price of Poole's water undertaking, and six others in the area, being amalgamated into a newly constituted Poole and East Dorset Water Board. The board, which was established in 1960, had nine members appointed by Poole Borough Council and nine appointed by the other member authorities, including the county council. It supplied in excess of 2,500 million gallons a year to a population of more than 132,000 in 330 square miles of the county. Poole received no financial consideration for transferring to it all the assets of its own water undertaking, apart from the transfer of debts of a little over £100,000.

The council, forseeing the demise of its own undertaking, purchased from it land which had long become surplus to requirements. One of these holdings was at Constitution Hill, where the Corporation in earlier days had constructed a reservoir to hold sea water, pumped from the Quay, that was used to cleanse roads and flush sewers. Another was at Hatch Pond, Waterloo, where a reservoir and pump house of the old Poole Waterworks Company had been situated, which was acquired by the Parks Committee.

None of these transfers was contentious, except for the Waterworks Committee's decision to abandon Poole's ancient well at Tatnam. The power to 'set one conduit head at Totnam' had been given to the town by Henry VIII in 1542, but it had been surrounded by railings and left unused for many decades, becoming a breeding ground for mosquitoes and flies. Development had reached the area, and nearby residents were happy at the proposal to fill it in, but the Society of Poole Men was outraged that such an historic monument should be lost to the town. However, in the middle of the argument, the developer of nearby houses produced a title to the ownership of the land, which had been accepted by the Land Registry. The council was able to claim that it no longer owned the well, and gave the owner permission to build over the site, subject to the well being drained!

*The old Tatnam Well.*

*'Poole Corporation Waterworks, Tatnam Well.*

*This ancient well, the property of the Poole Corporation marks the site of the conduit head, erected by the Mayor, Corporation, Burgesses, and inhabitants of the Town and Port of Poole in the 34 year of the reign of King Henry VIII, anno domini 1542, in order to provide themselves with additional supplies of water'*

*Plaque on the wall of Tatnam Well.*

*The old Tatnam Well.*

# Upton's Royal Residence

Contemplating the constant stream of visitors, of all ages, who today find peaceful enjoyment and relaxation among the wide lawns and secluded walks of Upton Country Park, it may be hard to imagine a time when the property was described as a white elephant so far as Poole Borough Council was concerned.

As mentioned elsewhere, a similar description was applied by the National Trust to the castle which it was given, along with Brownsea Island, in 1962. It was a building in need of maintenance which the Trust was glad to dispose of on a lease for a very modest sum. A similar fate at first attended Upton House and its surrounding grounds, which were given to the borough in 1957 by the Llewellins, the last family but one to occupy them as a private residence.

*(Above) The lawns and gardens became overgrown during the years that Upton House was unoccupied. It was hoped the house and gardens would be restored during Prince Carol's tenancy.*
*(Left) An early photograph of the rear of Upton House.*
*(Below) The interior of Upton House in its prime as a family residence.*

*The spiral staircase leading off the main entrance hall.*

They were to be followed, after an interval of some four years, by a couple describing themselves as Prince Carol and Princess Jeanne of Romania; but even the small rent fixed by the council, which could find no better use for the property at that time, was not a sufficient cushion against the financial embarrassments that were to befall the new occupants. After four years of litigation, Prince Carol had in 1957 won a declaration in a foreign court that, as the son of ex-King Carol II by a marriage that was later annulled, he was legally entitled to inherit a share of his fortune, said to be worth many millions of pounds. To the local tradesmen eager to supply the royal household, that was

*Prince Carol of Romania, 1962.*

probably a matter of less immediate importance than a reasonable expectation that bills would be settled promptly, just as servants would look to the Prince and Princess for regular payment of their wages.

Again, as with Brownsea, an ongoing and sometimes public controversy, involving the occupier of an important property and those who felt aggrieved by that person's attitude to certain responsibilities or privileges, would prove to be another passing show until an undoubted moment of destiny could arrive. In the case of Upton House, that moment was some two decades away when, in 1956, Mr William Llewellin first offered the property to the borough.

In the early Fifties, much of the land to the north of Upton House consisted of farms, smallholdings, nurseries and heathland. Creekmoor was a village of definitely rural character, by comparison with the rather more urbanised Broadstone. Both saw themselves as in some ways quite separate and distant from Poole; yet by the time Mr Llewellin made his offer, it was already clear that they would eventually be absorbed by the borough's expansion. It was also clear that the existence of what is now Upton Country Park would then become of enormous benefit to these areas.

Mr Llewellin, too, had an eye to the future, when he sought outline planning permission for houses, shops and business premises on 426 acres of land at Upton. When it eventually accepted the gift, the council refused consent on the ground that the land was not zoned for development. There was also no provision for sewerage. In fact, before reaching these decisions, the Corporation had been urging Dorset County Council to accept Upton House as a youth centre, in exchange for Planefield House, Waterloo, where it needed land on which to extend the sewage works at Broadstone.

Through no fault of its own, the council seemed fated from the outset to lay itself open to accusations of ingratitude and insensitivity. That was doubly unfortunate, for the Llewellin family had lived at Upton since 1901, and was highly regarded for a record of public service and integrity that made it one of the most distinguished to be connected with the borough in the 20th century. Mr Llewellin had bought a property in Bere Regis and was anxious to move out. He felt the borough had kept him hanging about for a reply. But the Youth Committee of the county council was not in favour of the exchange of properties: and so the borough decided not to accept the gift. Shortly before he left to visit his brother in Rhodesia, Mr Llewellin added some land to his offer, and said he would agree to some housing development, to offset the cost to the council. Several more months passed before the council reluctantly accepted the house, subject to covenants regarding its maintenance for the next forty years, together with 54 acres of farmland. George Rendle, the caretaker and gardener, who had been in the service of the family since 1935, became a council employee: and there, for a while, matters seemed to rest.

Toward the end of 1957, there were negotiations with the naturalist, Gerald Durrell, who wanted to establish zoological gardens to provide a sanctuary for endangered species. Mr Durrell, then living in Bournemouth with a collection of several hundred animals, described his plans at a news conference in the Zebra snack bar - named not in honour of wildlife, but because it was opposite Poole's first pedestrian crossing of this kind, in High Street. Once again, the problem would be the borough council's view of the future. Mr Durrell wanted to establish a charitable trust, along the lines of the Severn Wildfowl Trust. The Corporation wanted a tenant who would take the property off its hands for fifteen years or so, while the town grew nearer to it. In the end, Mr Durrell decided to establish his zoo in Jersey.

George Rendle reckoned that he showed more than sixty people around the property before it was eventually let. Ideas put forward for its use included a convent, a nursing home, an official residence for the mayor, a health resort, school, golf club, yachting centre, and mental hospital. After two years without finding an offer it could accept, the council itself, anxious to be rid of a maintenance bill of £1,500 a year, thought of seeking planning permission to use the 60-roomed house as a hotel, with holiday chalets and caravans in the

*George Rendle, the long-serving custodian of Upton House.*

grounds. It could hardly have been the sort of thing Mr Llewellin had in mind when he decided to offer it to the borough.

Nor, presumably, could he have dreamed of it becoming a 'royal residence,' which was the suggestion made to the Town Clerk in May 1961 when Princess Jeanne called at Poole Municipal Buildings to inquire on behalf of her husband about leasing or buying the property. The former Miss Williams was the adopted daughter of an American banker. She was born in 1930 and became the second wife of the 41-year-old Prince Carol in 1960. He had a teenage son by his first marriage to a Parisian opera singer. The Prince, previously known as M. Mircea Lambrino, lived for many years in Paris with his mother, formerly Magda Lupescu, and had worked as a bookbinder. After his mother's death in 1953 he commenced the lawsuits which led to his recognition as a legitimate co-heir with ex-King Michael, his father's son by a second marriage. The story of his recent past certainly sounded romantic, and his distinguished profile was allied to a diffident charm: but although she revealed that her husband could speak eight languages, it was Princess Jeanne who did most of the talking in public.

The rent the council asked, for the house and 27 acres of land, was one hundred pounds a year, rising after two years to four hundred pounds. It was hardly a king's ransom, but the terms of the 21-year lease made the Prince liable for repairs to the property, including the roof, on which, it was estimated, £20,000 needed to be spent. The assumption was that he would bring it up to a standard appropriate to an official residence and that it would revert to the borough in good condition at a time when the future of that area was much more settled.

It was felt that letting the property to Prince Carol was more in accordance with the wishes of the Llewellin family, but that was not how a number of citizens saw it. Charles Simmonds, the militant secretary of Parkstone Pensioners' Association, said the house had been given to the people of Poole. He asked what the council thought it was doing, giving it to a 'redunant Prince' when his members had waited two years for more public seats in Upper Parkstone. There was a wave of support for Ronald Bateman, the Isle of Wight zoo proprietor, who complained that he had been 'pipped at the post' by the Prince. Mr Bateman wanted an initial rent-free period and a long lease, but claimed a zoo at Upton House would have been attracting up to half a million visitors within a few years. Poole's Member of Parliament, Sir Richard Pilkington, joined in the debate on the side of the council, saying he could not believe that the critics really represented the spirit of Poole.

To understand the passions aroused, it is worth recalling that the British fervour for royalty was much greater in those days, while public opportunities to see members of the Royal Family were much fewer. Thus the visit of Princess Alexandra in May 1961, to open the new maternity unit at Poole General Hospital and lay the foundation stone for a new ward block, had been long and eagerly anticipated. This deep need for contact with royalty, even of a surrogate nature, was one that Prince Carol and his wife were able in part to satisfy. Their first public engagements were sometimes on a modest scale. At the Grand Christmas Bazaar of the Inskip League of Friendship for the Disabled, held at Hamworthy in December 1961, they arrived in a private hire limousine, driven by Mr Jock Campbell, who was later to be numbered among their creditors. Members of the organising committee were waiting to be presented to them, to the accompaniment of a *Pomp and Circumstance* march played on a small gramophone, before a speech of welcome by the Deputy Mayor, Alderman Bill Cole.

By then the Prince and Princess, and a comparatively small amount of furniture, were in occupation at Upton House. Even before they moved in, the Princess found herself in the local headlines, when she gave birth three weeks prematurely in the new maternity unit. She had been visiting Upton House to make arrangements for the move. In the early hours of September 1st 1961, the day the lease began, she telephoned the Town Clerk to ask if he could recommend a doctor, as she was in pain from her pregnancy. Her son, weighing six pounds, was born later that night. She decided he would be known as Prince Alexander, or Alexandru, in honour of Alexander the Great, an ancestor of Prince Carol. The arrangements which it was said the Prince had made for the baby to be born in the London Clinic thus fell by the wayside.

'The news that the family are almost ready to move in,' the *Poole and Dorset Herald* reported, 'has brought a stream of traders to Upton House anxiously seeking royal clientele...Callers at Upton House are dealt with by a lady-in-waiting.' Such obsequious attention probably rankled with Parkstone pensioners still waiting for public seats, yet it was only typical of the enthusiasm with which the Prince and Princess were welcomed by their supporters. A local woman who had been a society photographer in Rome and London sent them a picture of the late Queen Marie of Romania, a bizarre character, who with her sisters had been among members of European royal families who visited Brownsea Island in the days of the Van Raaltes.

In February 1962, the lease to Prince Carol from the previous September was signed. The controversy over its terms had abated, and the royal couple were frequent and prominent guests at a wide range of civic and social occasions in the area, although there was sometimes a little uncertainty about the degree of precedence they should be accorded. Visitors to Upton House found that decorators had been at work inside, and the handsome entrance hall looked bright and welcoming, yet there were few of the trappings of royalty that an excited public imagination may have come to expect. Any hopes George Rendle may have entertained about a squad of gardeners assisting him to bring the grounds up to stately home standards remained unfulfilled; and that was not to be his only disappointment.

Rumours about the way matters were in fact progressing at Upton House had begun to reach some members of the council. The Town Clerk was unimpressed by the Prince's statement that he had been surprised to discover, from the trustees of his inheritance, that capital could not be spent on current costs, such as maintenance, although it could be used for purchasing the house, which the council did not want to sell. It nevertheless came as a surprise to many people when the Finance Committee, in May 1963, recommended that the lease should be terminated on the ground of non-payment of rent. The amount owing, about £40, did not seem a large sum for such drastic action, but at an annual rent equivalent to less than £2 a week, it represented a substantial period of arrears, probably much longer than would have been allowed, in those days, to the tenant of an ordinary council house. The arrears had been paid off before the recommendation came before the full council meeting, so it was withdrawn.

Public attention of a different sort was now focussed upon the couple. At a charity garden party a few weeks later, guests noticed that the usually immaculately attired Princess appeared in badly laddered stockings. In August

*Princess Jeanne and the young Prince Alexandru on the lawn of Upton House.*

the issue was taken up by the Communist candidate in the council by-election at Broadstone, where he managed to poll 42 votes. He held what would now be called a photo opportunity at the gates of Upton House, at which George Rendle claimed he had not been paid for some time.

In her reply to this attack the Princess, as was often the case, produced an explanation which hinted at loftier concerns, telling the *Herald*: 'We helped organise an anti-Communist conference in Paris some years ago and then went on a world tour speaking against Communism. These are probably repercussions from that time.' It is not recorded whether the unsuccessful Communist candidate, a plant operator from Alderney, was flattered or baffled by any suggestion that his campaign might have made him a catspaw of the KGB.

In reply to national newspaper allegations that Mr Rendle had not been paid for 26 weeks, and that the Princess ran up a bill of more than £400 with a local grocer, she explained that their own money did not come in regularly, but that they were not poor. 'How can people say we have not got any money when we have spent thousands of pounds decorating and improving this house?' she demanded.

How, indeed? Councillor Fred Rowe, whose company was involved in carrying out the work, declared he could vouch that it had been done. Four years later the company commenced bankruptcy proceedings against the Prince, which were withdrawn on payment of the balance of a £2,000 bill for decorations. In September 1963 Ernest Lees, the administrator of the royal household, decided to leave. His wife had sometimes been introduced as the Princess's lady-in-waiting. The situation was not made any easier when Mr Lees decided to make public a letter which it was said emanated from the household of ex-King Michael of Romania. This document denied, somewhat petulantly, the Prince's right to his title, although after his long legal battle, it could not do other than acknowledge him as among the heirs of King Carol II, albeit in the name of Mr Mircea Gregoire von Hohenzollern, formerly Lambrino. It was, however, in the name of Prince Carol that he was sued in Poole County Court the following March by Margaret Milne, the former nanny to Prince Alexandru, for the return of money lent and arrears of salary. Her claim for £202, and the Prince's counterclaim for £52 mesne profits and the return of a gold ring, were settled before the hearing.

The saga of Upton's royal residence was to continue for a few years more, until 1969, when the Prince moved out, and the council was obliged to accept that there was no point in pursuing legal action against him for arrears of rent, rates, insurance premiums and repairs for which he was liable under the lease, which could have amounted to £10,000.

*'The reduced rent for two years was to help pay for extensive repairs. In fact, we are paying nearly £1,000 a year: £250 rates and an insurance policy for £80,000'*

*Princess Jeanne.*

# The Poole Corporation Act, 1961

Two-storey beach huts and better catering facilities at Sandbanks; a parade of stalls on the corner of Old Orchard to help meet the needs of hungry visitors to Poole Quay; and a requirement for every house in the borough to display a street number: these were among the consequences that flowed, directly or indirectly, from the passing of the Poole Corporation Act, 1961.

As finally presented to Parliament, the borough council's draft Bill ran for 68 pages and contained 137 clauses. As it was the first Bill the council had promoted since the 1938 Poole Corporation Act, it also sought to incorporate a number of extra powers which other local authorities had obtained since then.

The Corporation was restricted by covenants on where it could build on Sandbanks recreation ground, as well as to the height of buildings and the size of any car park, and its powers to regulate trading on the Quay were insufficient. There was no power to invest money from the council's superannuation fund in shares in companies. The council also wanted to be able to spend money it was then receiving from the sale of corporate properties on completing the Civic Centre buildings, without requiring Ministerial permission.

The Bill was deposited in Parliament in November 1960, and its promotion was approved, first by the council, and then by a public meeting of local government electors at the Municipal Buildings, the following month. There was some concern expressed at the public meeting about the section which sought to give the council powers to suspend restrictive covenants on land it wished to acquire, but the Town Clerk explained that the intention was only to get rid of covenants which were 'archaic and pretty well pointless.'

There were other sections in the Bill which may have owed something to the expansionist mood of the time. One sought powers to establish and manage an aerodrome undertaking: another, which sought powers to run a golf course and zoological gardens, foreshadowed plans for the land being reclaimed at Baiter. It was also proposed that the Sheriff of Poole should receive an allowance for official duties in his, or her, own right, and not as a subvention from the Mayoral allowance; and that the council should be able to spend money on preserving buildings of architectural interest. At the request of the police, it also included a cause requiring window cleaners to register with them, as a crime prevention measure against burglars adopting that pose.

The Bill was first introduced into the House of Lords in March 1961, when a committee under the chairmanship of Lord Merthyr considered its contents, and the opposition it had attracted, and 135 clauses survived this scrutiny.

A Ministry of Health representative opposed a clause to ensure that all milk sold in the borough was pasteurised, and other clauses dealing with public health matters. In regard to these, the committee noted that if the Public Health Bill then before Parliament was passed, thirty-two clauses of Poole's Bill could be withdrawn.

The Bill had its First Reading in March and its Second Reading in April 1961. Then there was considerable negotiation to reach agreement with various Government departments, statutory undertakers, and other public bodies, so that petitions against the Bill could be withdrawn. One petition sought to require the council to notify all owners and tenants of property in the Sandbanks peninsula of its proposals for development on the seafront. When this procedure was complete, it became an unopposed Bill for consideration by a committee of the House of Commons, at which officers of the Corporation gave evidence in support of its proposals.

The clause requiring householders in the borough to mark their homes with a number easily visible from the street was proposed in an endeavour to help the emergency services and other callers: but in the committee room, it was seen almost as an affront to civil liberties, and drew strong criticism from the chairman, Sir William Anstruther-Gray. 'Why should people be compelled to do something they don't want to do?' he demanded. 'I cannot see any need for this particular provision at Poole in advance of other parts of the country.'

John Barron, Poole's imperturbable Borough Engineer, produced photographs of properties to illustrate the problem, and mentioned the Branksome Park area as a particular example. All the council was asking, he said, was that the street number should be put on the gatepost. It would be a great help to postmen and doctors.

'A postman should learn his job and know the houses,' retorted Sir William. 'If he doesn't know them he should not be a postman. If an ambulance driver cannot find a house then it is only the person in the house who suffers. I am not favourable to this clause.' There was much that might have been said, in reply to these comments, on the issues of helpfulness, humanity and plain common sense, but Mr Barron would not be drawn into such a confrontation. 'We are only trying to be logical,' he answered.

Sir William moved to his next point. What if a householder objected to putting up the number 13? Would the council take him to court for that? 'We have had this number 13 matter every time on house numbering,' Mr Barron replied, 'and the Corporation has agreed to 11a, or something of the sort, to get over it. We are merely asking that the number should be visible from the street, so that people, including the police, ambulance men and doctors, can find the place quickly.'

*Robert Leggat, Poole Borough Council's chief public health inspector (centre), oversees the removal of a caravan from Canford Heath.*

'It is a poor policeman,' Sir William observed, 'that doesn't know one house from another.' But when he consulted his colleagues on the committee, he found that they did not support him on the issue of house numbering, and the clause was allowed to remain. So was another, giving the council power to deal with squatters, vagrants and others encamped on Canford Heath. Robert Leggat, the chief public health inspector, said fences had been torn down and landowners were at their wits' end, even though the council had been moving families off the heath at the rate of about ten a week.

The amended Bill went back to the House of Lords in July and received its final reading in the Commons the same month. It received Royal Assent in August 1961.

The council now had power to deal with a situation on Poole Quay that had continued virtually without legal restraint since a decision by the borough magistrates that the Quay was not part of the seafront within the meaning of the 1938 Poole Corporation Act. This had opened the way for an invasion of the quayside by a wide variety of stallholders and market-type traders, whose wares and activities ranged far beyond the time-honoured, and perhaps rather sentimental, vision of humble fishermen selling their catches to passers-by. In the words of Alderman Bert Stokes, chairman of the General Purposes Committee, it had become 'more or less a fairground.' Yet it was this traditional perception of trade on the quayside, with another hint of civil liberties being infringed, that would add to the difficulties of enforcing the 1961 Act.

The Act gave the council powers to prohibit the sale of any goods on the Quay, other than fish from fishing boats. It was anxious to make use of them, because the frequently rubbish-strewn state of the quayside was a matter of public concern, and the police had difficulty in clearing stalls out of the way so that ships could discharge cargoes. As well as obstructing the legitimate interests of trade on the Quay, the stalls were seen as unfair competition for established businesses nearby.

A total ban on such trading, however, proved impossible to achieve. The operators of two shellfish bars and an ice-cream stall exercised their right to appeal to the borough magistrates against refusal of permission, and the result was something of a compromise. The appeals were allowed, subject to a number of conditions about hours of trading, siting of the stalls and vehicles, and a review of the position in three months' time.

Maurice Yeatman, Clerk to Poole Harbour Commissioners, who was called as a witness on behalf of the council, said that trading from stalls had increased since the railway lines were removed from the Quay, allowing more car parking. His words are evidence, also, of the change that has since occurred in official attitudes towards tourism and the Quay. 'The Commissioners have supported the council's refusal,' he said, 'because they don't want the public encouraged to the Quay. The town is becoming more and more a holiday resort, and unfortunately, the Quay is one of the main attractions for holidaymakers - whereas it isn't for their use at all.' It was not desirable for them to walk about near ships being worked.

In 1963, the council gave permission for one ice-cream stall and one seafood bar to trade on the Quay. A second ice-cream trader was successful in an appeal to the magistrates; but Mrs Jean Matthews of Skinner Street, who claimed her family had been fishermen in Poole for four centuries, lost her appeal against refusal of permission for a seafood stall.

Mrs Matthews became known as 'the Portia of Poole' after making a further appeal to Poole Quarter Sessions, where she conducted her own case and won the sympathy of the Recorder, Malcolm McGougan, who commended the great skill and care with which she presented it. Allowing the appeal, he said he had given considerable weight to the possibility that inshore fishermen might suffer unless such an outlet was available to them.

Private enterprise was to provide the ultimate solution to the problem by erecting a row of permanent stalls at the corner of the Quay and Old Orchard, into which some of the most vociferous opponents of the council's ban on quayside stalls were to move, and subsequently prosper.

# The Civic Centre

Civic pride and ambition were rising in Poole during the early nineteen-sixties to the sort of levels known in the years between the two world wars, when many municipally inspired developments, both in the town and along the seafront, seemed also to express an air of celebration and delight with its heritage.

For many years, and indeed until this day, the Municipal Buildings at Park Gates East have handsomely fulfilled their role as a focal point for Poole's sense of pride in its history and achievements, among which they deserve to be numbered themselves.

They were begun in 1931 when the borough council, having obtained the approval of the Unemployment Grants Committee, complied with the condition that work should commence with three months, by having the foundations laid by direct labour.

The building was designed by the then borough engineer, Mr E J Goodacre, and his staff, and in May 1931 the Lord Mayor of London laid the foundation stones. By May of the following year the new buildings were ready for their official opening by the Earl of Shaftesbury. Including the specially designed furniture, they had cost £62,900.

*The Municipal Buildings. The entrance hall. The Conference Room is to the left in the photograph.*

Despite the relatively short span within which the buildings were designed and erected, there had been time to incorporate many local and historical references into their internal and external features. For instance, the enriched ceiling bands of the Council Chamber were designed to suggest shells, rhododendrons and a dolphin motif, with the Mayor's and Sheriff's chains of office introduced as carved ornaments on the oak panelling of the walls. Original stained glass from Sir Peter Thompson's house in Market Street was used in the frieze windows, while other stained glass panels depicted many aspects of the town's activities. Significant dates in civic life through the centuries, such as the granting of charters and other rights and privileges, were commemorated in the ceiling decorations, around the rim of the domed skylight. There were very many such internal features of this kind, including mosaic floors by Carters, while on the exterior of the buildings, twenty-four stone panels, designed by Percy Wise, then head of Poole School of Art, illustrated important events in Poole's history.

The original vision had been on an even grander scale, of a civic centre to incorporate all the fountain-heads of local administration. It would have stretched all the way round the block of land bounded by Commercial Road, Park Road, Sandbanks Road, and the road at the rear of the Municipal Buildings, and included a Town Hall with an imposing facade.

Though this dream of civic splendour was destined to remain only as a rough outline, the reality by the nineteen-fifties was that the Corporation's staff

*The Municipal Buildings. The first floor. The Council Chamber is to the left in the photograph.*

*The Council Chamber looking towards the entrance. The public galleries are on each side.*

*The two Committee rooms could be converted into a single room.*

*(Above) The 'Picture Gallery' on the second floor.*

*(Left) Park Road was quiet enough for a swan to saunter across when the Crown Buildings were under construction at the Civic Centre site, 1962.*

and its judicial duties had outgrown the Municipal Buildings. The 'Conference Room' had to serve as a courtroom for the Magistrates, the Recorder and the County Court, as well as for public inquiries, town planning appeals and public meetings. The problem was made more acute because it had been a condition of the grant with which the Municipal Buildings were built that one wing should be let to Her Majesty's Inspector of Taxes for Poole. The vision of a civic centre, however, remained.

In the early nineteen-fifties the council decided that all Corporation departments should eventually be housed in such a centre, and it began to acquire large private houses which fronted on to Sandbanks Road, Park Road and Commercial Road. Most were at first converted into offices, pending their eventual redevelopment. Some of the land facing Park Road was sold to provide a site for the Crown Buildings, so that Government offices would form part of the civic centre, and HM Inspector of Taxes could vacate a wing of the Municipal Buildings.

Poole had had a Court of Quarter Sessions since its Charter of 1568, and an unbroken line of Recorders since that date, with the exception of the years 1643-1650, when the Recorder of Poole was suspended on suspicion of siding with the King.

On a few occasions during the Victorian period, the Recorder had been presented with a pair of white gloves, to signify that there were no cases for him to try, but in the middle of the twentieth century, this was far from being the case. In 1962, for instance, the Court of Quarter Sessions sat for 39 days, and tried 108 cases, in which 153 prisoners were involved, as well as hearing 16 appeals from the Magistrates' Court.

In 1954 the Magistrates suggested to the borough council that the long, voluntary service of Poole's Recorders should be commemorated by the erection of a plaque in the Conference Room, which was then used as a courtoom.

The council agreed, and invited the senior ex-Recorder of Poole, the Rt Hon Lord Goddard, Lord Chief Justice of England, who had been Recorder from 1917 to 1924, to unveil the plaque.

On the afternoon of 26th November 1954, after lunch at the Haven Hotel, a procession including the Lord Chief Justice, Sir Mervyn Wheatley, HM Deputy Lieutenant for Dorset, and all those involved in the administration of justice in the borough, together with members of the council, walked from Central Police Station to the Municipal Buildings. The band of the Dorset Regiment was playing on the forecourt, and there was a guard of honour in the foyer.

In the Conference Room, the Lord Chief Justice formally unveiled the plaque. His speech was followed by remarks from three former Recorders of Poole, F S Laskey (Recorder of Salisbury), H Elam (Deputy Chairman of the

County of London Sessions) and H J Phillimore (Recorder of Winchester); and by the Recorder of Poole, Malcolm McGougan; the Mayor, Alderman Fred Reeves, and the Member of Parliament, Captain Richard Pilkington.

The need for improved clinic services in Poole had been under discussion since 1946, and the council agreed that the first new building on the civic centre site should be the Central Clinic, which was erected on the corner of Sandbanks Road and Park Road. It was to take much longer merely to obtain approval for this building than it took for the approval, design and construction of the original Municipal Buildings. Dorset County Council was involved in some of the services to be accommodated at the clinic, and there were restrictions on capital spending to be overcome. The project was finally agreed in 1957. Work on its construction began in June 1960 and was completed in April 1962. The design won the private architects, Farmer and Dark, a Civic Trust Class I award for Dorset. The citation stated that 'by compact planning and skilful use of the sloping site, the architects have produced a beautifully detailed building which respects the scale of its suburban surroundings and provides a positive contribution to the visual improvement of the environment.'

The Central Clinic's purpose-built accommodation made it possible to close down about half a dozen separate clinics that had been housed in older and less adequate premises in various parts of the borough, and bring them under the same roof.

*(Left) Lord Goddard, the Lord Chief Justice of England, 1954. He was Recorder of Poole 1917-1924.*
*(Centre) Malcolm McGougan, Recorder of Poole, 1954-1974.*
*(Top right) Henry J Phillimore, Recorder of Poole, 1947-1954.*
*(Middle right) Henry Elam, Recorder of Poole, 1941-1947.*
*(Bottom right) Francis Laskey, Recorder of Poole, 1939-1941.*

# Homes on the Heathland

Greater emphasis on individual home ownership; an end to the building of council houses; and the opportunity for many more people to acquire a property of their own for a relatively modest outlay, were familiar themes of housing policy in the Eighties. They were already part of Poole's vision of the future in the nineteen-sixties.

At the start of the decade the borough council still had some 2,000 people on its housing waiting list, despite the great progress that had already been made with new council estates. The forecast was that such developments would cease by the mid-1960s, when the proportion of council housing in the borough would have risen to about 20 per cent. The council felt that was as far as it could go.

Early in 1961, on the completion of programmes at Turlin Moor and in the Old Town, the council agreed that Canford Heath was the next area in which housing would be provided.

Hundreds of acres of the heath were used during the second world war as a military range and training area, and during the nineteen-fifties there had been a number of accidents involving unexploded missiles. In 1959 Poole's Member of Parliament, Captain Richard Pilkington, raised in the Commons the need for effective action by the War Office to make the heathland safe, after its de-requisitioning. There had been two serious accidents on successive days during June 1958, in which two boys threw an unexploded mortar bomb on to a bonfire, and three other boys unearthed a missile and stoned it until it exploded.

The Member of Parliament demanded a further detailed search of 626 acres of the heath which were regarded as the most dangerous, but the Under-Secretary of State for War (Mr Hugh Fraser) declined, in view of other commitments. He said there was no evidence to justify further action, when more recent discoveries on the heath had proved to be only harmless parts of exploded mortar bombs. Such accidents as did occur, he declared, were nearly always the result of people - especially young ones - fooling about with unexploded missiles. But he undertook that an officer from Southern Command would be available to investigate any suspicious objects turned up during building work on the heath.

Canford Heath at that time was still a relatively remote and unexplored area. Its boundary with the main built-up area of Poole to the south was the recently built Old Wareham Road, linking the main roads to Wimborne and Ringwood that roughly defined its other boundaries. The small farms and other holdings that once lay between the heath and semi-rural areas of northern

Oakdale had already begun to disappear. Ernie Gale, who at the age of 68 in 1954 still worked a smallholding in Old Wareham Road with 11 cows, 26 pigs and 150 chickens, was one of only seven smallholders remaining in the area. There had been more than twenty when he was a young man.

During 1962 the council purchased 228.5 acres of the heath from various owners, but mainly from Lord Wimborne, at a cost of £437,000. It considered that developing the land itself would offer many advantages over piecemeal private development. It would allow the Corporation to develop it as a whole and provide sites for new houses at a reasonable cost, as well as recouping the high cost of off-site works which otherwise would have to be borne by the ratepayers. It also felt that an estate providing some 1,400 houses and bungalows over the following five or six years would have a stabilizing effect on land and house values.

This was the prospect held out by Alderman Bravery, chairman of the Estates Committee, in 1960: 'We are prepared to make land available so that people can buy plots. They will be available at very low deposits - they should be somewhere about £25. Then they can build their own houses and always have somewhere for themselves.' The council would provide mortgage facilities, giving preference to applicants from existing council houses or those already on the waiting list. Hundreds of hopeful home-owners wrote to the council to register their interest in such a scheme.

The undeveloped cost of the land was less than £2,000 per acre. The council conveyed 21 acres to Dorset County Council, for use as playing fields, in exchange for a similar area at Planefield House needed for extension of Broadstone sewage works. A further seven and a half acres were sold to the county council as a site for new school premises.

There was, though, much work to be done before there could be any thought of building houses. High-voltage electricity pylons had to be re-routed, and off-site sewers laid over private land. The council's decision that all services would be laid before any land was offered for sale meant making arrangements with local gas, water and electricity boards. Post Office Telephones laid all their wires underground to serve the first part of the estate.

The council's objective was to develop an integrated neighbourhood, with homes for sale at minimum deposits, from which it could recoup its capital investment, estimated to reach £1.06 million, as soon as economically sensible. As well as the school and playing field sites, other areas were earmarked for shopping and community facilities, open spaces, and tree belts.

Having appointed its first Borough Architect, Geoffrey Hopkinson, in 1960, the council was able to plan the new development as an integrated neighbourhood, and to provide well-designed houses for sale at reasonable prices. It felt it was essential that the new area should be seen as a natural outward growth of the town, and not severed from it by a major traffic route. An underpass was therefore designed to give the estate a direct access to the rest of the town. The contract to build it was given to Holdyne Limited for £53,500. Work began in May 1963 and when it was completed the following year, Old Wareham Road would be taken over the underpass by a three-span bridge one hunded and seven feet long.

The snow and severe weather of early 1963 brought work on the laying of roads and services to a standstill for seven weeks, and delayed the sale of the first stage of the development. Before then, however, concern had also been growing about the problem of the heath's existing unofficial population of gipsies, travellers, squatters, and others who lived in an assortment of caravans, tents, shacks and sheds.

Dr James Hutton, Poole's Medical Officer of Health, had reported in 1960 that it was becoming increasingly difficult to deal with them under existing legislation. 'They are determined not to leave the neighbourhood,' he said, 'but to live under the most primitive conditions on the outskirts of the residential areas, where they are a nuisance and a menace to the community from their anti-social habits and behaviour.'

Calls for effective action to deal with long-standing grievances about the heath-dwellers were repeatedly heard in the council chamber, but Alderman Donald Haynes, chairman of the Health Committee in 1961, rightly observed that they were now part of a national problem, because it made no sense merely to move them out of the area of one local authority into another.

Similar sentiments were expressed by a local resident in Poole Magistrates' Court when he spoke on behalf of five caravan-dwellers who were prosecuted by the council for failing to abate a nuisance. The council alleged that the defendants were living in squalid conditions on a site off Old Wareham Road that was only one hundred yards from occupied houses. By May 1962 Ronald Vivian, a lay preacher, of Hythe Road, had become the gypsies' champion and spiritual leader.

It was a scene that might have come from the pages of Thomas Hardy. Clasping a large leather-backed Bible, his hair tossed by the driving wind and rain, Mr Vivian stood on the tailboard of a truck and led his motley congregation of heath-dwellers in prayers for the council. Members of Heatherlands Gospel Hall led the hymn-singing. The previous day the gipsies had sent a telegram to the Queen appealing for help to find somewhere to live. They had nowhere else to go, so they had moved back on to the heath, only a few days after the council carried out a mass eviction.

Led by the chief public health inspector, Mr Robert Leggat, the eviction involved towing vans on to the grass verge on the opposite side of Old Wareham Road. A similar operation was carried out on land at the rear of the

*(Above) Only a small police presence was required to maintain law and order during the eviction of heath-dwellers from land adjoining Old Wareham Road.*

*(Below) Caravans and belongings were deposited on the grass verge after their owners had been evicted from Canford Heath on the opposite side of Old Wareham Road.*

Alderney council estate by men acting on behalf of Lord Wimborne. It says something for the more orderly nature of life in those days that the total police presence amounted to a dozen officers, two vans, and a patrol car.

By November 1962, the cause of the heath-dwellers had also been taken up by the self-styled 'Gipsy King,' Tom Jonell. From a flatlet in Parkstone Road he proceeded to launch the Human Development Foundation, with an ambitious fund-raising target, to rehabilitate the national gipsy population, who it was claimed had become outcasts in modern society. As the *Poole and Dorset Herald* drily observed, no doors were barred when Mr Jonell called at the Mayor's Parlour, for his quest was not for old clothes, but for six million pounds. The Member of Parliament for Poole, Sir Richard Pilkington, as he had now become, was named as vice-president of the foundation.

The obvious solution to the problem was to find the gipsies somewhere else to live, but the council's plan to create a permanent site for up to twenty caravans on land in Roberts Lane, Creekmoor, had to be dropped after furious protests from local residents. There was a similar furore about an alternative

*Life could be hard for the heath-dwellers. This woman and her son lost most of their belongings when their caravan caught fire.*

*Young people - and their pets - at a typical encampment on the urban fringe of the heath.*

*A television camerman is allowed in close to film a bomb disposal operation on Canford Heath, which could still be a fairly relaxed occasion in the 1960s.*

site in a disused railway cutting off Willett Road, Merley, while an offer by Councillor Fred Rowe to provide a camp site on a chicken farm between Verwood and West Moors was no more welcome in that area.

The council, meanwhile, was anxious to proceed with its development at Canford Heath. In May 1962 Mr C D Pilcher, of Graves, Son and Pilcher, of Brighton, was appointed to advise on the best method of disposing of building plots to individuals or local builders, on which to erect one of the house types designed by the Borough Architect. Contracts to buy and develop the first stage were advertised.

In May 1963 the council accepted a tender of £130,000 from Ruddock and Meighan Limited for the first stage, which would provide 127 homes, at prices expected to range from £2,650 to £4,250. Construction work was due to begin in September 1963, but the council's search for a suitable site for the gipsies remained fruitless. It therefore resolved to abandon the search and remove about twenty families of caravan-dwellers from the land. A fence was built along the Old Wareham Road frontage, and the stage was set for the second forcible eviction within eighteen months.

The encampment of some twenty-seven adults, seventeen children and sixteen caravans was evicted in a matter of hours in October 1963, the remaining gaps in the fence were closed, and those who stayed by the roadside in Old Wareham Road, or tried to move to council land at Turlin Moor, were ordered to move on. A week later, a few caravans were back on the heath at Haymoor Bottom, about a mile from the nearest water supply.

It was a defiant stand by the travellers. On another part of the heath, homes were being completed at the rate of one a day, and a show house was being prepared for its official opening by Dame Evelyn Sharp, permanent secretary to the Ministry of Housing, whose sympathy with the council's efforts was often instrumental in obtaining the Minister's consent to the grant of loan sanctions.

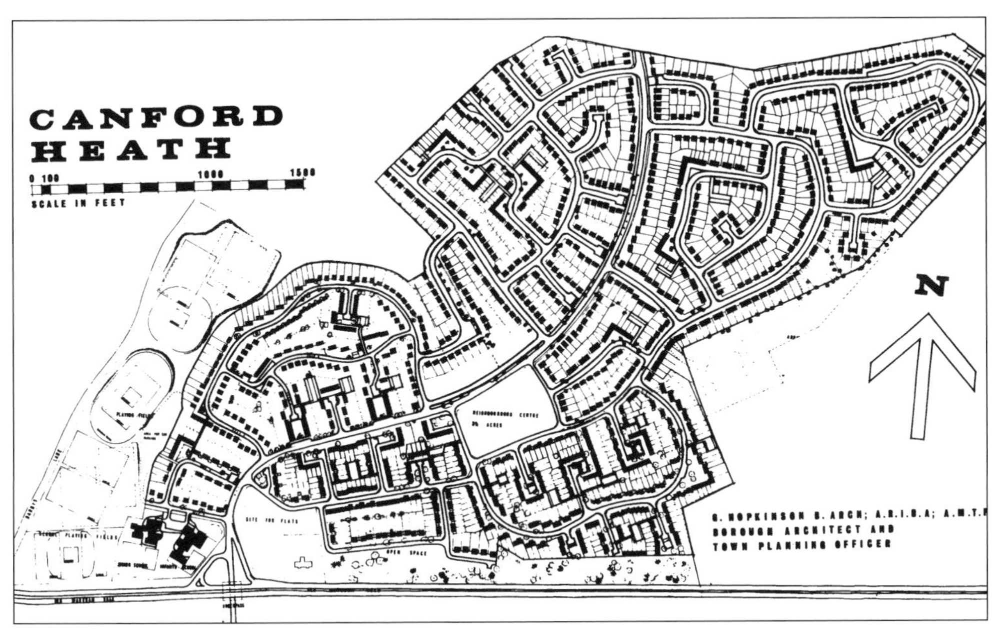


*Plan of Canford Heath development.*

*Bernard Short, Borough Librarian and Museum Curator, retired in 1955 and Leonard Shaw was appointed in his place.*

*Population in Poole in June 1961 was 90,960.*

*The Corporation agreed to take over the Hunger Hill Burial Ground when it was officially declared to be a Disused Burial Ground and the land was levelled and the land declared an open space after the tombstones had been removed to the perimeter of the land.*

# Amenities and Open Spaces.

## Libraries & Parks

Public demand for books to read increased constantly throughout the decade, thanks to the success of new branch libraries provided by the borough council.

Between 1946 and 1953 the Libraries Committee had opened branch libraries at Broadstone, Newtown, and Canford Cliffs. In 1957, using a prefabricated classroom, it provided a service at Oakdale. The following year it was able to extend services at the Central Library, after Poole School of Art moved to the Guildhall. Responsibility for the school had earlier been transferred to Dorset County Council.

Bernard Short, the borough librarian and museum curator, retired in 1955. In 1962 his successor, Leonard Shaw, was able to report that more than one million books had been borrowed from Poole's libraries that year, compared with 630,000 in 1953.

Adjoining the Central Library in South Road (now Lagland Street) was Poole Museum, which in 1962 attracted 28,000 visitors. It regularly received gifts and offers for sale of exhibits with local connections, but the town's lack of an art gallery was one reason why the Libraries Committee refused an offer from Australia of a portrait in oils of Samuel Clark, an old Poole merchant, who was mayor in 1812. Also declined was a marble statue of John Joseph Norton, a former timber merchant and freeman of the borough, whose benefaction had in 1887 provided the premises in South Road as a free library and school of art. However, the committee did accept from the artist Bernard Gribble, who lived in Parkstone, a gift of eight coloured drawings, painted in 1750 from Raphael's original designs for the Vatican, of which the only other set was in the South Kensington Museum. It also accepted from Mr Courtenay Dickinson the gift of a large 120 oz silver soup tureen and ladle which was presented to his grandfather in 1886 on his retirement from the office of town clerk.

The committee was also responsible for Scaplen's Court, the medieval town house and former guildhall in High Street, which was reopened to the public in May 1959. It had been closed, as being structurally unsound, in November 1950, but the council, with the approval of the Ministry of Works, had subsequently carried out an extensive programme of reconstruction work, as funds permitted. In 1959, 6,851 visitors paid the admission charge of one shilling (5p) for adults, or sixpence (2½p) for children. It remained open from May to September each year, and by 1962 the annual total of visitors had nearly doubled, to 13,524. There were exhibitions of pottery and photographs, as well as a maritime exhibition, staged in co-operation with the Society of Poole Men.

The council's Parks Committee had an easier time than the Libraries Committee, as it was able, during the decade, to increase its income as well as to add appreciably to the town's open spaces and recreational facilities. There were also major contributions from private enterprise, such as the opening to the public of the restored Compton Acres gardens at Canford Cliffs, and the establishment of a ten-pin bowling centre on the site of the old Woodman Hotel in Poole Road, Branksome. Compton Acres, a series of seven unique ornamental gardens, had been laid out before the war at a cost of about £220,000, and had been on the market, in a neglected state, for some four years when their rescuer appeared in 1950. Mr John Stanley Beard, a retired architect, had the gardens ready for their official reopening in May 1952, and by 1961 they were attracting more than 85,000 visitors a year.

*Rockley 'looking west' at the time of the Corporation's purchase. Access to the track leading to the point was obtained from Lake Drive and through the land which became the Royal Marines camp.*

# Rockley Sands Holiday Camp

As early as 1951 the land facing Poole Harbour at Ham Common has been included in the Poole development plan as a site for a holiday camp, but it was not until 1952 that the borough council gave the Parks Committee the go-ahead. The council had earlier felt that some of the land might be needed for housing if the Admiralty would agree to sell the derelict wartime shore establishment, *HMS Turtle*, that lay to the north.

The site envisaged for the holiday camp was of some 58 acres surrounding the lake formed by the abandoned Doulton's clay pit. The eastern end was accessible, albeit with some difficulty, from Napier Road. However, Lord Rockley, the owner, was unwilling to sell part of his total holding of 128 acres at Ham Common, because it would leave the rest completely landlocked by the Admiralty's land, overlapping any possible entrance being constructed from Napier Road.

In the hope that it could acquire land from the Admiralty to provide an entrance to the rest of the estate, the council agreed to purchase all Lord Rockley's land at Ham Common. The purchase included the pier and pipeline leading to the RAF's underground tanks in the hillside, from which the airfields of Dorset had been supplied with fuel during the war. Meanwhile, the Admiralty decided to establish an amphibious warfare training centre for Royal Marines on the site of *HMS Turtle*, and required exclusive use of the lake for training members of the Special Boat Squadron. Their operations were surrounded with secrecy, which meant that during some exercises the public would also have to be excluded from areas overlooking the lake.

As a result of negotiations with the Admiralty, it was agreed that the Corporation would grant a licence to the Admiralty to use the lake, and change its holiday camp site to the hinterland, and that the Admiralty would convey a strip of land, sixty feet wide, to give access through its land, and pay for the construction of 1,400 yards of road from the end of Napier Road to Rockley Point. It was also agreed that the road would be aligned so as to allow the building of officers' houses along it, and that in return for connection to the public sewerage system, the Admiralty would convey six acres of land including the old sewage works of *HMS Turtle*, which the Corporation would dismantle.

Some years earlier, the chief superintendent of the Military Engineering Experimental Establishment (MEXE) at Christchurch had expressed interest in carrying out research into soil stabilisation on Ham Common, which was the only sizeable area it could find in the West Country which had silt soil covering a gravel capping. As a result, the Brigadier in charge of MEXE needed little

*(Top) Rockley beach at the time the corporation purchased the land. The purchase opened up nearly a mile of harbour frontage. (Inset) The landing stage near Rockley point.*
*(Below) Ald. Lloyd-Allen, Mrs Stone, Mrs Lloyd-Allen, George Stone, Alex Levy, Mrs Butler, Ald. Bright, Mrs Hillier, John Hillier at the opening of the Administrative Centre, Rockley, 1957.*

*(Top) The harbour from Rockley Point*
*(Below) The Palladium, Rockley Sands.*

persuasion to build the new road for the Corporation, subject only to the Corporation being responsible for providing materials and night watchmen. In fact, helped by the Territorial Army in Portsmouth, and with the loan of bulldozers and other heavy equipment, MEXE excavated, filled and reshaped the new road, stabilised the soil, and surfaced it, during February and March 1956.

The Corporation, meanwhile, had decided to offer some fifty acres of land for the formation of the holiday camp, and provide thirty acres of public open space, including the harbour frontage of nearly a mile. The lake was let to the Admiralty, with power to exclude the public from a surrounding area, totalling about fifty acres, when the lake was being used for amphibious exercises.

Four of the applicants for the lease of the holiday camp site were interviewed by the Parks Committee. The formal lease to Mr Alex Levy, who with his solicitor, Mr George Stone, formed a company, Rockley Sands Limited, to develop the site, was signed in March 1956. The following month, the Mayor opened the new road, and development of the estate could commence. The agreed rental was £2,500 a year, increasing by £2,500 a year to a total of £10,000, and the programme of development provided for the camp to be completed by 1960.

In 1961 it was found necessary to construct a swimming pool, and a further 0.65 of an acre was let to the company, and the lease extended to 99 years, for an additional rent of £1,600 a year.

The costs incurred by the Corporation were:

| | | |
|---|---|---|
| Land | | £14,373 |
| Site expenses | | 291 |
| Road, lighting, drainage | | 13,170 |
| Pumping station | | 4,885 |
| Pumping station machinery | | 1,535 |
| Electricity cable | | 1,012 |
| Total | | 35,266 |
| Less | | |
| Admiralty contribution | 9,593 | |
| Rockley Sands Limited | 272 | 9,865 |
| Net cost | | £25,401 |

By 1962 the Corporation had received £46,000 in rent, and Rockley Sands Limited had paid £35,000 in rates, more than £20,000 of which had gone to Dorset County Council.

# Turlin Moor

The Central Electricity Generating Board had obtained the Board of Trade's certificate allowing it to dump silt from the excavations for Poole Generating Station at sea. It therefore felt that a similar approval would be given for the dumping of fly ash from the coal-fired generating plant. At the first suggestion of such a prospect, Bournemouth Corporation registered strong opposition, fearing that sea dumping might harm its bathing beaches. Bournemouth's objections were immediately supported by the borough councils of Poole and Christchurch.

It was already late in the day, and negotiations were not going well, because the board, assuming that permission for sea dumping would be granted, raised the matter only months before the generating station was due to come on stream. It was said that the barges required had already been ordered. At this point, when Poole's representatives observed that sea disposal would hardly be an option for an inland power station, the board offered to show them how the ash was being used to reclaim land at Swindon.

The Corporation was impressed by the scheme, and agreed to buy eighty-three acres of mainly swamp land at Turlin Moor, Hamworthy, which could be filled with ash and eventually form a new recreation ground. Under an agreement with the Corporation, the board undertook to pipe the great amount of surface water running on to the land to discharge in Lytchett Bay; to build a bund along the frontage to the bay, to prevent the seepage of ash into the harbour; and to fill the land to a depth of seven feet six inches, later reduced to four feet six inches.

Between 1953 and 1959, this agreement was meticulously observed. Ash and clinker from the generating station proved ideal for the purpose. Between five and seven acres of land were filled each year and returned to the Corporation for seeding. In fact, many other uses for the ash were found. Considerable quantities were used to raise the level of land for the new sewage works at Broadstone, and at Bushell Mill Farm for the construction of Old Wareham Road. Other quantities were sold to builders for the same purpose, or for the manufacture of breeze blocks, while 15,000 cubic yards were diverted to Southampton for use in the building of Marchwood power station. In those years the supply of ash seemed inexhaustible, particularly when two additional coal-fired boilers were installed, but in 1959, the Government ordered the station to convert to oil firing.

By then, nearly thirty acres of swamp land had been reclaimed, and half of it grassed and laid out for recreation. By 1961, all the reclaimed land was in use, five football pitches had been formed, and a temporary wooden pavilion erected. Plans to provide an athletics track and pitch-and-putt golf course were approved the following year, but Government curbs on capital spending meant that the Corporation was refused sanction to borrow the £19,000 needed for the scheme.

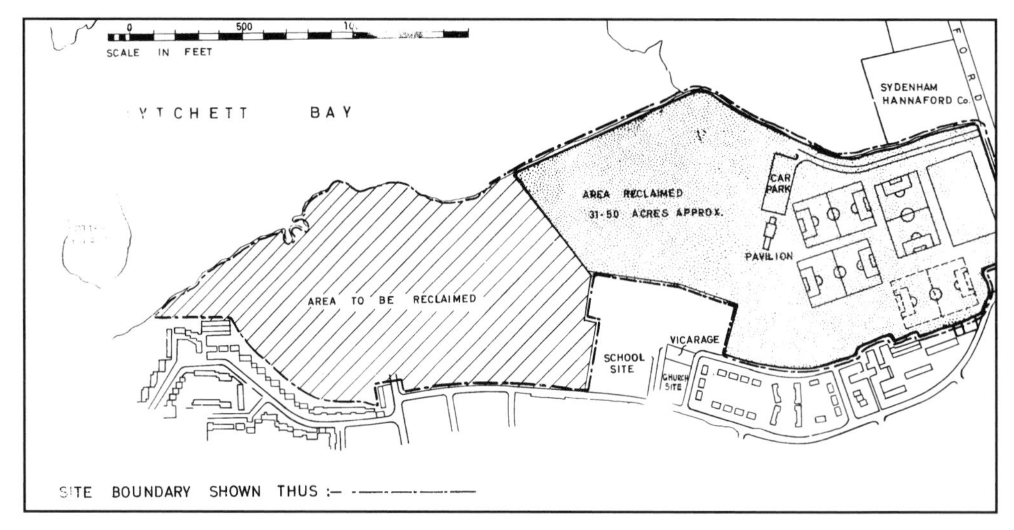


*Plan of Turlin Moor reclamation.*

*Poole Park in the winter of 1962-3.*

# Poole Park

The Parks Committee of the borough council was responsible for Poole Stadium, the Rockley Sands holiday camp development, and reclamation at Turlin Moor, as well as for recreation grounds, open spaces, parks and beach facilities.

By 1963 it had nearly 600 beach chalets which were let to local residents and produced an income of £25,000 a year, with another 176 chalets under construction. Business was good on the seafront in post-war years, when foreign travel was still severely restricted. Poole's beach facilities brought in a further £20,000, of which £8,000 came from the hire of wooden deck chairs and sun traps, in the days before so many visitors brought their own.

Poole Park, however, remained the jewel in the committee's crown, and it was by its management of the park that it was most widely judged. The cricket pitch and outfield were well enough resuscitated for Dorset County Cricket Club to play two of its Minor Counties fixtures there each year. Even more illustrious names were in action in the park as early as 1953, when a former Poole entrepreneur returned to the borough in some style, as the host of a party which included Test cricketers from three nations.

R T A Cornwell's XI had been brought together by the son of a Poole Alderman who was enjoying an unprecedented period of prosperity in his business life. 'Ronnie' Cornwell, whose own son, David, is better known by his *nom de plume* of John le Carré, always appeared to have his heart in the right place, if not his funds, as le Carré's portrait of him as Rick Pym in *A Perfect Spy* implies:

> *The burden is that any money passing through Rick's hands is subject to a redefinition of the laws of property, since whatever he does with it will improve mankind, whose principal representative he is. Rick, in a word, is not a taker but a giver and those who call him otherwise lack faith.*

In the summer of 1953, however, so many notable cricketers felt able to accept Mr Cornwell's invitation to appear against a Poole Park XI that it was agreed that each team would consist of twelve players.

Among them were Sidney Barnes of Australia, Learie Constantine and Roy Marshall of West Indies, J M Parks of Sussex, and D N Silk, of Cambridge University, who later became President of MCC. It was reported that 8,000 spectators came to the park. They were hugely entertained by a one-day match in which 453 runs were scored. The Poole Park XII did well. It could almost have claimed a moral victory, for it dismissed eight of the visitors by the time

*The new railway station of the model railway in Poole Park.*

they had scored 259 runs and, when stumps were finally drawn, it had scored 194 for the loss of only three wickets.

The park's tennis courts were also popular, while its bowling greens were considered good enough for the final rounds of the National Triples Championship in 1958. In 1959, Poole Model Yacht Club held its first national radio-controlled yacht regatta at its headquarters near Whitecliff railway arch. Bands were hired to play in the park on summer weekends; an area was set aside for a children's zoo, which opened in June 1963 with a collection of some one hundred and twenty birds and animals; and artists were encouraged to stage summer open-air exhibitions. The park's miniature railway acquired its own station. Ten Canada geese were released on to its lakes by Dorset Wildfowlers' Club. A poster hoarding site and a derelict cottage in Parkstone Road were acquired to establish a rose garden, and there were plans to move the Parks Department nurseries to another site in order to extend the area of open space. But this proposal, like one to replace the railings around the park - lost to wartime appeals for metal for the munitions industry - failed to obtain Government sanction for the expenditure involved.

By the mid-fifties, the lack of maintenance during the war years began to make itself apparent. The drains of the cricket pitch silted up, and Dorset county match umpires declared the outfield unfit for play. The fresh water lakes had to be dredged, and on one occasion lorry-loads of dead fish had to be removed from the salt water lake. The explanation then given was that they had been starved of oxygen during hot, dry weather by the growth of marine organisms, which formed a film on the surface of the water. At first it was thought that the lake should be left to fill and empty with the tides during the winter; but then it was found that a new sluice was required at the inlet beneath Whitecliff railway embankment.

The problem of increased traffic on the park's roads was not solved by shutting Middle Gates and Norton's Gate to vehicles. That did nothing to reduce the speed of traffic, which was considered a danger to children and pedestrians, or relieve the congestion caused by a lack of parking space for visitors.

To counteract the speed problem, the council invoked an old byelaw which restricted the speed of vehicles to eight miles an hour, and although no prosecutions were brought for speeds under fifteen miles an hour, there were twenty-one prosecutions in February 1953 and forty-two the following month. The committee flirted with the idea of prohibiting traffic altogether, but decided that would cause parking problems elsewhere, as well as robbing many people of the opportunity to visit the park. A scheme to increase the amount of parking also fell by the wayside. The committee felt that with a salt water lake of more than sixty acres, compared with less than forty acres of open space, it would be reasonable to reclaim an area on the eastern side of the lake for a car park: but this scheme was rejected by the council after opposition from residents.

When the park was first formed, the ownership of the salt water lake was in doubt. It was in reality part of Parkstone Bay, and had become virtually enclosed only by the construction of the railway embankment. The Corporation had done its best to safeguard the use of the lake by taking a licence from the Crown Commissioners and obtaining a lease from Lord Wimborne of such rights as he might possess over it. After an indecisive interview with the then Viscount at which the Corporation offered to purchase these rights, the council made a compulsory purchase order. It eventually the acquired them for £500.

In 1960 the council finally obtained Government approval to borrow £32,000 to build a new café that would replace the old tearooms in the park. Work was delayed five months by a shortage of steel before it was completed and let to Anthony Forte, who named it Swan Lake. One-third of the building was operated as a restaurant, and the rest as a cafeteria. The two sections were separated by a partition which could be drawn back to accommodate larger functions.

The first such function, an opening night dance organised in December 1961 by Poole and district branch of the National and Local Government Officers' Association, was observed, through the curtains, by a police inspector. The police were concerned that under the current licensing laws the restaurant licence for the premises required that the supply of alcoholic drink was ancillary to the service of substantial meals. The borough magistrates had granted an occasional licence until midnight, but had stated it was not to be regarded as a precedent.

Details of the police observations were given to the magistrates when the Swan Lake's licensee applied for an occasional licence to serve drinks at a company dinner dance until 11.45pm. They accepted Chief Superintendent Jack Gray's contention that drinking for approximately one and a half hours before, and again after, the service of a meal was not ancillary to it - and after hearing that dinner would be served between 7.30 and 8.30pm, granted the extension from 7.15 until 8.45pm!

*Swan Lake café, Poole Park*

*(Above) The earlier café, Poole Park.*

*(Below) Swan Lake café, Poole Park facing the freshwater lake.*

*An aerial view of Poole Stadium.*

# The Stadium

## FOOTBALL

In 1953, Poole Town Football Club was promoted to Division II of the Western League, at the start of what was to be one of its best periods of achievement.

The club was the successor to Poole Football Club, which played on a ground off Fernside Road until it went into liquidation. Poole Town Football Club was formed to play at the Stadium, where in 1953 its lease was renewed by the borough council, at a rental of seven and a half per cent of its takings, plus £92 per a year for the catering rights. The council helped with the provision of floodlighting and the club prospered. In 1955 it was promoted to Division I of the Western League, and Stan Rickaby, a former England full-back, was appointed manager.

One of Rickaby's colleagues had been Wilf Mannion, known to the tabloid press as 'the Golden Boy of English soccer', and to others as its stormy petrel. In 1955, Mannion was having contract problems with his club. Hull Football Club thought it had signed Mannion to play for it, but Mannion thought differently, and was without a club to play for when his old friend Rickaby persuaded him to join Poole Town. With two nationally famous players on its staff, and all the publicity of the quarrels between Mannion and the other clubs, it began to attract gates of 5,000, which had never been seen before. It was not long, however, before Mannion fell out with Poole Town as well, considering that a fee of £20 a match was hardly worth his journey to the Stadium, and in March 1956, he did what the local press described as 'a midnight flit.' The club's fortunes had been nevertheless given a lift, and in 1957 it won the Western League championship and was promoted to the Southern League.

Meanwhile, Poole Town Football Supporters' Club had established a local football pool, in which prizes, often reaching £1,000 a week, were paid to subscribers who chose matches ending in a 3-3 draw, or the team that was first to score 13 goals. One hundred and fifty part-time collectors were appointed, and, eventually, there were said to be 30,000 weekly subscribers. The club used its profits to support the football team, paying over between £6,000 and £10,000 a year during the nineteen-fifties.

Despite these considerable subsidies from the Supporters' Club, the team's performances fell away, and in 1960 it had a disastrous year, ending only one place from the bottom of the Southern League Premier Division, with a new manager who refused to resign his contract, and directors who were interviewed by the Football Association in connection with alleged illegal payments to players, whom the press characterised as 'shamateurs.'

However, with a new manager, the club recovered its poise with part-time players in 1961. Leonard Matchan became chairman of the club, and with money provided by the Supporters' Club, a £35,000 stand was built, which Sir Stanley Rous, secretary of the Football Association, formally opened in August 1961.

The following year was the club's best. Its part-timers fought their way into the first round of the FA Cup. Poole Town was drawn at home to Watford, holding it to a draw before a crowd of 9,000 at the Stadium. The Mayor and many leading Poole people joined Sir Mervyn Wheatley, the club president, for the replay at Watford, where Poole lost only narrowly by two goals to one.

## *SPEEDWAY*

Leonard Matchan, who played a part in reviving the football club's fortunes, had earlier been involved with speedway racing at the Stadium. Mr Matchan, a Labour councillor and parliamentary candidate, found an unlikely partner in Geoffrey Bravery, a fellow member of the borough council who was also chairman of Poole Conservatives. They took over as promoters from Clifford Brewer, who started speedway racing at the Stadium in 1948.

Meetings were held each Wednesday evening during the season. The 'Pirates,' later taken over by Southern Sporting Promotions, drew around 6,000 spectators to each meeting. The Poole team prospered, with locally recruited riders, such as Ken Middleditch and Brian Crutcher, being chosen to ride for England. In 1955 the Pirates were champions of the second division of the Provincial League for the second year running. They were promoted to the first division, where they became champions in 1961 and 1962.

## *GREYHOUND RACING*

In 1959 the borough council, after consulting nearby residents, agreed to let the right to operate greyhound racing at the Stadium to Southern Sporting Promotions, a company headed by Charles Knott of Southampton, where it already operated a track. The lease was subject to the company forming a track, erecting a stand, club room, restaurant and totalisator facilities, and would pay the Corporation a rent of £1,600 a year, rising to £2,000. Racing commenced on 8th May 1961 and meetings were held on Monday and Thursday evenings. Poole was the first new racecourse to be accepted for operation under National Greyhound Racing Club rules since 1947.

Official Programme
COPYRIGHT
1/-

Tel.: POOLE 1220

**POOLE GREYHOUND RACING Co. Ltd.**

**Greyhound Racing**

DIRECTORS
CHARLES KNOTT, [illegible] PETTY, Tote Direction.
LICENSED BY AND RACING UNDER THE RULES OF THE NATIONAL GREYHOUND RACING CLUB
RIGHTS OF ADMISSION RESERVED

**1st Meeting - Monday, May 8th, 1961**

**1st RACE — 480 YARDS FLAT — 7.30 P.M.**

**1 Red — LUCKY BOY** — S.S.P. Ltd. — J. Appleby
bd d by Lucky Fair—White Orchid (January, 1958)
May 1 Tr. 2 480 Trial 6th to Knockrue 10 L 30.70 G 57¼
May 4 Tr. 1 480 Trial 2nd to Count of Chippelgaun 1 L 30.76 G 57¼
May 5 Tr. 1 480 Trial Won 30.20 G 57¼

**2 Blue — CASTLEWRIXON BOY** — S.S.P. Ltd. — J. Appleby
bd d by Lucky Fair—Summer Glare (May, 1958)
May 1 Tr. 5 480 Trial 2nd to Black Magourna 2½ L 30.25 G 62
May 4 Tr. 1 480 Trial 2nd to Porteous Again ½ L 29.91 G 62½
May 5 Tr. 3 480 Trial 3rd to Noted Hero 13 L 30.68 G 62¾

**3 White — PORTEOUS AGAIN** — S.S.P. Ltd. — J. Appleby
be bd d by Violin 'Cello—Greenlawn Lass (January, 1959)
May 1 Tr. 3 480 Trial 2nd to Knockrue 4½ L 30.27 G 62½
May 4 Tr. 3 480 Trial Won 29.90 G 62
May 5 Tr. 1 480 Trial 2nd to Untouchable 7 L 30.42 G 62

**4 Black — COUNT OF CHIPPELGAUN** — S.S.P. Ltd. — N. Appleby
bd d by Chippelgaun—Lucky Hunch (September, 1959)
May 1 Tr. 1 480 Trial Won 30.80 G 63
May 4 Tr. 4 480 Trial Won 30.70 G 62
May 5 Tr. 1 480 Trial Won 30.60 G 62

**5 Yellow — SMASHING MEMORY** — S.S.P. Ltd. — N. Appleby
bd d by Victory Song—Memories of Home (November, 1958)
May 1 Tr. 2 480 Trial 3rd to Black Magourna 3½ L 30.31 G 66
May 4 Tr. 6 480 Trial 3rd to Count of Chippelgaun 3 L 30.88 G 65
May 5 Tr. 6 480 Trial 2nd to Lucky Boy ½ L 30.23 G 65½

**Reserve — RYAN'S MAGPIE** — S.S.P. Ltd. — T. Appleby
b d by Second Harvest—Ryan's Lassie (June, 1957)
May 4 Tr. 6 480 Trial 4th to Porteous Again 4½ L 30.15 G 66½
May 5 Tr. 6 480 Trial 3rd to Untouchable 10 L 30.60 G 66½

RESULT—
1st..........
2nd..........
3rd..........
Time..........
Won by
..........lengths
DIVI'S
WIN..........
1st P..........
2nd P..........
FORECAST
..........

*Above) Race card for the first greyhound race meeting at Poole Stadium, May 1961.*
*(Left) The new stand erected at the stadium when greyhound racing was introduced.*

## *FAIRS*

Poole had held two fairs each year since Henry VI gave the town his licence in 1453. For many years thereafter farmers, corn merchants, horse-dealers, clothiers and tinsmiths had come each year from nearby counties, to set up their booths, together with traders in wines and clothing from France and Belgium. A great deal of business was done, and to encourage visitors, entertainers of all kinds, such as jugglers, dancers and bear-baiters, would provide 'all the fun of the fair.'

The May fair had died out by the 18th century, and the main business side of the November 'All Souls' fair failed in the following century, so that only the entertainment side remained. During the nineteen-fifties, the right to hold this fair on the Stadium car park was granted for five-year periods, and Mr Gilham's bid of £1,500 a year was successful.

# The Cultural Scene

Poole's determination not to go on living in the shadow of its neighbour, Bournemouth, developed on a broad front from the early nineteen-fifties. But there was so much catching-up to do that no local authority, however far-sighted and ambitious, could have afforded to tackle every issue at once.

The habit of looking to Bournemouth for many of the functions and services that Poole could not provide was already deeply ingrained, perhaps no more so than in the field of culture and entertainment. How, in any case, could a dormant seaport presume to compete with a famous holiday resort whose town centre boasted a Pavilion, a Winter Gardens, and a thriving Little Theatre, not to mention a symphony orchestra that, against all the odds, managed to survive after the mass sacking of the Bournemouth Municipal Orchestra in 1954?

Poole clung grimly to its ironic tourism slogan that 'the best parts of Bournemouth are in Poole' while its young people took buses across the borough boundary to enjoy many kinds of entertainment they never expected to find in their home town, which ranged from American big bands to summer shows starring the most famous names in British show business. Even new films were quicker to reach the screens in Bournemouth after their national release: and the homespun charms of Poole's Regent, Regal and Amity could not compete with the plush interiors of Bournemouth's biggest cinemas in Westover Road or the Lansdowne.

There was no denying that Poole people were as capable as any of creating the spirit of enthusiasm and fellowship that is needed to drive the cultural life of a community. They had shown it in 1952 with the outstanding success of the Pageant of Poole, and it also made itself felt whenever the ancient ceremony of Beating the Bounds of Poole Harbour was performed: but there was nowhere for it to grow. And so in 1954, less than two years after its formation, the Poole Pageanteers' Association was disbanded. Wilson Kenyon, the Town Clerk, who chaired the final meeting, hoped there would be some event in the future which would rekindle the energies and enthusiasm of the Pageanteers; but it was not to be. Former Pageanteers could only look on enviously while, in the neighbouring village of Lytchett Minster, Madeline, Lady Lees managed to involve almost the entire population of 2,500 in the making of a Gospel film, *Voice in the Wilderness.*

In 1959 Poole's oldest cinema, the Amity in High Street, was sold as a site for a new Woolworths store. The cinema manager, Walter West, had been there since 1926, five years before it showed its first 'talkie.' At one time the cinema had an orchestra of six musicians to accompany silent films. It was

*(Above) The Regal Cinema, Ashley Road, Parkstone.*
*(Below) Some Enchanted Evening for Bert Wilcox and Phyllis Hayes in Poole and Parkstone Amateur Operatic Society's production of South Pacific at the Regent Theatre.*

built in 1882, originally as a public hall, by the Odd Fellows, and was still remembered by an older generation as the Amity Palace of Varieties. Like the Regent Theatre, at the Longfleet end of High Street, and the more recent Regal Cinema in Ashley Road, Parkstone, it was owned by Capital and Counties Electric Theatres, which also owned the Electric Theatre in Bournemouth and cinemas in Wimborne and Romsey.

The company's managing director was Alderman Geoffrey Bravery. It was formed in 1919 by his uncle James Bravery. During the summer of 1963, the grant of planning permission to redevelop the sites of Electric and the Regal was followed by the sale of all the company's five remaining cinemas to Allied Land and Investments of London. It was a matter of some concern, not only to local cinemagoers, but to the Poole and Parkstone Amateur Operatic Society, whose shows had been staged at the Regent since 1927. Herbert Cobb, the society's chairman, anxious that the Regent's continued survival now appeared to depend upon 'the success of the combination of films and bingo,' added his voice to those already calling for the provision of a public hall that was suitable for a wide range of community activities. Among them was Alderman Bert Stokes, president of the newly formed and highly successful Poole and District Camera Club.

Poole's Deputy Mayor, Alderman Wilfrid Haskins, acknowledged these sentiments, declaring prophetically: 'A new town hall is a thing we would all like, but it is a thing which will cost a lot of money and will never pay for itself when it is up.'

During the same year, the lack of a suitable hall or gallery was again highlighted by the bequest to the borough of 75 paintings by the celebrated marine artist Bernard Gribble, who died at his home in Parkstone, at the age of 89, in 1962. 'Poole now has what every town seeking county borough status should have - an art collection,' observed the *Poole and Dorset Herald*. But a suitable home for it was still needed.

Broadstone, a district long noted for its spirit of self-help, had already met its own needs for a community hall. Since June 1945 a committee had been in existence to raise funds for a suitable memorial to the victims of the second world war. A clock tower in the Broadway, or a bungalow for a disabled ex-soldier, had been suggested, but in 1954, it was decided to erect the War Memorial Hall. The borough council agreed to grant a 99-year lease of the site. Building started in 1956, with the aid of a grant from the Ministry of Education under its village hall scheme, and the hall was officially opened the following year. It included a kitchen, a large stage, and dressing rooms, and became the new meeting place of several local organisations, including the Broadstone Players.

The Players were thus more fortunate than many of the other amateur drama groups that flourished in the town. The facilities they were able to enjoy

*Bernard Charles, potter and ceramic artist, who was one of the founders of Poole Art in Industry Association.*

in an assortment of church halls and similar buildings were usually quite modest. Some new school halls had stages that were much better equipped, but their out-of-town locations, and the restrictions imposed on their use, made them unattractive to amateur companies.

Artists, designers and craftsmen working in the area also felt the need of a focal point for their activities. Led by Bernard Charles, a pottery teacher, they formed Poole Art in Industry Association, with the aim of establishing a better platform in the area for the cause of industrial design. One of the association's first projects, supported by both the borough council and Poole Chamber of Trade, sought to revitalise the Quay end of High Street by means of colour co-ordinated decorations and other improvements to the street scene, along the lines of a Civic Trust experimental scheme in Magdalen Street, Norwich. The council sponsored a meeting between High Street traders, the Civic Trust, and the Art in Industry Association, and offered its support. Although one shopfront was redecorated, to serve as an example of what could be achieved, the scheme failed to attract the support of the required minimum of 80% of traders, mainly because so many High Street shops were branches of multiple retailers whose shops had their own distinctive style.

In 1961, when the Southern Gas Board offered to sell Beechurst, the Georgian mansion on the corner of High Street and South Road, to the borough council, after being thwarted in plans to demolish it, the association suggested that it might be converted into an arts and design centre. With neither project able to come to fruition, however, the organisation failed to survive. It became a region of the Design and Industries Association in 1962, but was dissolved the following year because of poor support and lack of funds.

Shortage of funds had been a problem for the Bournemouth Symphony Orchestra ever since it arose from the ashes of the Municipal Orchestra, which was disbanded by Bournemouth Borough Council in 1954 as being too costly to subsidise at the ratepayers' expense. Despite the formation of the Western Orchestral Society as its new management body, and its promotion as 'the orchestra of the West,' approaches to neighbouring boroughs for help were not always well received. Councillors were inclined to ask what was in it for their part of the world, or to compare the requirements of culture with the demand for main drainage, in debates whose length could be out of all proportion to the contribution being sought.

In anticipation of the first of those questions, the Western Orchestral Society undertook to provide concerts in the areas of authorities who supported it through the Western Authorities' Orchestral Association. Here again, the lack of a suitable venue might have been a considerable problem, had not the orchestra, and those in charge of it, proved so adaptable. As a result of Poole's support for the orchestra, it gave its first ever concert in the borough, conducted by Charles Groves at St James's Church in 1960. The choir, from the Dorset Guild of Singers, overflowed from the chancel into the gallery, so that Mr Groves also had to conduct singers who were high above his head on either side of him. The church organist, Norman Vick, who took part in the performance, could not see Mr Groves at all, and had to depend on another conductor to relay his directions. In retrospect, it was one of the first steps down a long road that was to lead the Bournemouth Orchestras, and the town as a whole, to a worthy new home for the arts at Poole Arts Centre.

*Leader Gerry Brown (trumpet) and Mike Blakesley (trombone) of Gerry Brown's Jazzmen play for fans at Bournemouth YMCA. The band was chosen as the support group for Louis Armstrong's All-Stars on their 1962 British Tour.*

*'The Guildhall should be turned into an Art Gallery'*

*Eustace Nash, artist, who lived in Gorsehill Crescent, Longfleet.*

*The 60ft high chimney of the East Quay Sewage Pumping Station, a landmark of Old Poole for many years, was demolished in 1960 when the steam pump was replaced by an electric one.*

Poole Harbour Office. Berthing master Bill Harvey has just returned by bicycle from his rounds.

# The Port and Harbour

Poole Harbour in the early nineteen-fifties still seemed sufficiently large and accommodating for all the varied activities connected with it to co-exist without conflict.

There were few demands for centralised control or co-ordination while the number of those fortunate enough to be able to exploit its 'air of strength and usefulness,' or to find solace and recreation in its peaceful backwaters, was relatively small, and they treated it with respect as a matter of course. Such administration as was required was mainly in the hands of a small group of long-serving and dedicated employees of the Poole Harbour Commissioners, who worked in the somewhat cramped and antiquated surroundings of the Georgian Harbour Office, on the corner of the Quay and Thames Street, under the penetrating gaze of the Harbour Master, Captain Caesar Horn, a retired master mariner of the old school.

There were few exciting cargoes among the modest tonnage or so that passed over the quayside. In a typical year, about one thousand coasters would enter the port. Coal for the gasworks, coal - and later, fuel oil - for the generating station, and petrol for the oil companies' distribution depots at New Quay and West Quay Road were among the main imports. About 180 ships a year brought timber, maize, and fertilizer, and there was a modest export business in barley, ball clay, and caravans. The relatively shallow depth of water at Poole Bar, and in the shipping channels, which limited the size of vessel that could use the port, seemed to be accepted as a natural barrier to its commercial expansion, and despite the great increase in imports due to the generating station, trade overall did not increase. Though it was large enough to provide comfortable livings for shipbrokers, agents, stevedores and other services connected with the port, there was little to encourage newcomers from elsewhere to break into its close-knit community.

The quays were still serviced by the railway, but importers would often unload ships directly into their own lorries, leaving the lines little used, with trucks left on them empty and apparently abandoned. The single three-ton electric crane owned by the Harbour Commissioners was also little used, and

*Young men take the Sunday morning air on New Quay, Hamworthy, August 1962. The gasworks coal gantry on Town Quay was still in use.*

on occasions stevedores from Southampton had to be hired to help with unloading cargoes.

It might well have been that the Commissioners were inhibited as regards expansion of the port by the spread of spartina grass, which had mysteriously appeared and become rampant in the harbour. As the grass grew it collected mud and sand, making new little islands in shallower parts, and threatening the Main Channel, upon which much of the Commissioners' income was spent in almost constant dredging.

The Commissioners, presided over by the mayor of Poole, met in public every month in the first-floor boardroom of the Harbour Office. The room was hung with old charts and hydrological maps, and heated by a number of curious circular gas fires whose flues went straight through the ceiling. The ancient cane-bottomed chairs around the boardroom table were commodious, rather than comfortable; but that scarcely mattered, since the Commissioners often concluded their public proceedings in a matter of minutes. When the

*Though railway lines were still in use on Town Quay, many importers preferred to unload cargoes into their own transport.*

representatives of local merchants, fishermen, landowners, and public bodies connected with the port all knew each other so well in the course of day-to-day dealings, they tended to solve many of their problems as they went along: and the Commissioners appointed to represent Poole and Wareham borough councils were usually happy to leave them to it. It was a manner of doing business 'according to the custom of the town of Poole' that would not have seemed unfamiliar to the ambitious merchants and burgesses who had dominated the port in more prosperous days.

Commissioners were expected to act faithfully and impartially as trustees of the best interests of the harbour as a whole, and not as delegates of the body which appointed them. Continuity of tradition was seen as important in safeguarding these interests. This was perhaps symbolised when in 1963 the Commissioners acquired a site for a new boardroom from Poole Corporation. They purchased the former public library building at 4 High Street which had been built and presented to the town as a gift in 1833 by its Members of

Parliament, Benjamin Lester Lester and the Hon. W F S Ponsonby. In due course it was demolished and replaced with a new building of very similar layout to the old Harbour Office on the Quay.

At the conclusion of the war in Europe, the United States Coastguards, the US Transportation Corps, the Navy and the Marines had soon given up their bases in Poole, although it was not until 1948 that British Overseas Airways, having abandoned its seaplane services, finally withdrew from the harbour, which had been its marine base for eight and a half years.

By the nineteen-fifties, few of Poole's population were involved in, or depended upon, trade in the port. On the other hand, thousands thought of it as a vast recreational area for boating and sailing. Those who were not yachtsmen or fishermen themselves would be invited on board their friends' boats, or would join visitors on pleasure boats for a trip round 'the Lakeland of Dorset.'

Tradition and continuity were also symbolised by the ceremony of Beating the Bounds, which was reinstated in 1949 and held at three-yearly intervals. It united the main users of the harbour with a wider community around its shores. Mayors and Admirals of the port of Poole who set out on their official perambulations in 1952, 1955, and again in 1958 and 1961, were following in a

*In 1948 BOAC had abandoned its seaplane services from Poole Harbour and its aircraft, some of post-war production, such as 'Sandringhams' and 'Solents' with less than 10 hours' flying time were left in the harbour. A few were sold, the rest beached at the Royal Marine's 'hard' at Hamworthy where most were broken up. This photograph was taken in August, 1954 from Napier Road.*

*Seaplane at 'the hard' Hamworthy to be broken up. The ignoble end for Seaplanes which had flown all over the world from Poole Harbour in the war. They had flown over 5,000,000 miles without a single serious crash.*

*Olympic yacht racing in Poole Bay.*

*The Admiralty jury on their way by landing craft to the ferry steps at Shipwrights' Arms, for their inspection of the Broomhill boundary stone.*

tradition already more than four centuries old. Ever since 1526, when Henry VIII gave Poole Corporation exempt Admiralty jurisdiction over the harbour, and appointed the mayor to be Admiral of the port, it had been the Admiral's duty each year to swear in a jury of experienced mariners to peregrinate the bounds of the harbour and present to the court anyone who had infringed upon any part of it or been responsible for any untoward happening.

As early as the 17th century it had become the practice of the Admiral to arrange for the bounds to be beaten on the Whit Monday holiday, which allowed his colleagues and friends to accompany him on an enjoyable day out on the water. This enjoyment, however, was not allowed to detract from the serious business of the proceedings when the jury returned to Poole Quay and made its presentments to the Admiral, as regards both the use of the harbour and infringements of its rights. Byelaws might then be made on the matter, such as the size of fish allowed to be taken, or the periods when oysters could be dredged. On another occasion the Lord of the Manor was taken to task for erecting a jetty in the harbour without the Admiral's permission.

The Admiral's jurisdiction extended out from the harbour entrance into Poole Bay for about three miles. The distance had been defined as being as far as a person, standing on the shore, could see a 42-gallon barrel floating in the sea. It therefore took a jury some time to delineate the boundary and ensure that all was well in this part of the jurisdiction: and so it became the practice for the Admiral's party to land at Sandbanks, pitch tents, and pass the time with a meal and light-hearted games while awaiting the return of the jury.

A former town clerk, Richard Bramble, wrote a memorable account of such a perambulation in 1649, when the mayor's party stopped for refreshments under a tilt made from oars and sails at North Haven Point. The young men played a kind of football with their hats, and then

> *it pleased Mr Moses Durell, having Peter Hiley in his one hand, and John Gigger in the other hand...for a better and future remembrance of the claymeinge of the admyrall jurisdiction and liberties abovesayd, to lead these two youths in his hands about knee deep into the ocean...*

When the tide turned, they sailed back to Poole, where they took wine, beer and tobacco at Mr Melmoth's inn: and afterwards

> *every man taking his leave one of the other in a civil loveing and courteous manner, they departed to their severall and respective homes...*

More than an official record of the proceedings survives Richard Bramble down the years. His words tell something of the spirit in which the ceremony was performed. They have helped to encourage later generations of Poole citizens to a similar manner of observance, and to underline the importance of impressing on 'the younge men' those ancient traditions. Though a change in the law in 1835 meant that the Corporation was deprived of its Admiralty powers, the ceremony seems to have become so ingrained in the customs of the port that it was carried on for several years before it fell into disuetude, later being revived in 1921 as a picturesque water pageant.

Even the reclusive Mrs Mary Bonham Christie, living out her last years in defiant solitude amid the faded and overgrown glories of Brownsea Island, was prepared to respond to the spirit of such an occasion. She relaxed her rigid ban against visitors landing there, and welcomed a party of 'pirates' on the quayside. In September 1961, a few months after her death, her grandson John honoured the perambulation with a salute fired on the ancient cannon of Brownsea Castle, and a quarter peal of Bob Minimus on the bells of the island's Church of St Mary. It was the first time they had rung out since Mrs Christie's reign began in 1927.

The revived ceremony observed the old procedures. The jury was duly empanelled and sent by boat to the extremes of the harbour; children's hands were 'pricked' to ensure they remembered the bounds; but for the most part it was no more than a glorious water pageant as the vessel carrying the mayor, his chaplain, the aldermen and councillors, proudly flying the Admiral's burgee, accompanied the jury boat around the harbour, followed by a flotilla of vessels of all kinds, gaily dressed for the occasion.

There was, though, one addition to the old ceremony which added further excitement, in the form of a fearsome boatload of self-appointed 'pirates.' It

*(Above) Crowds line the quayside as boatloads of spectators prepare to join the Beating of the Bounds procession.*

*(Below) Beating of the Bounds, 1961. The Mayor, Alderman Mrs Elsie Hickinson, ceremonially pricks a girl's palm 'to remember the Bounds'.*

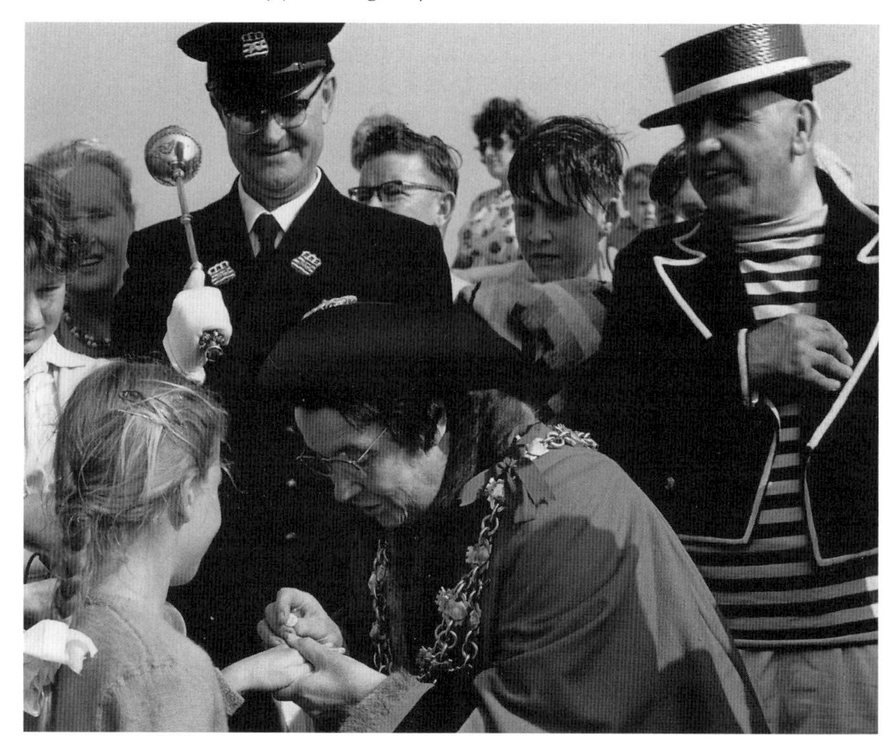

*The 'Pirates' stand by to board the Admiral's barge.*

*'Pirates' on the rampage in High Street before the ceremony of Beating the Bounds, 1961.*

became the custom for these colourfully-dressed and otherwise respectable characters to harass traders and innkeepers in the Old Town before taking to the water and attempting to raid every boat in the procession and demand money for charity. The pirates, after being captured by the jury, were made the subject of a 'presentment' to the Admiral, who sentenced them to walk the plank. According to Harry Ashley, a former 'pirate' and producer of the Beating the Bounds ceremony, nobody seems to know when they first became part of it. One tradition is that in the years between the two world wars some townsfolk, vexed at not being invited to the official perambulation, dressed up as pirates, took to the water in their own craft, and made a nuisance of themselves. Whoever was responsible, it proved to be an inspired addition to the pageantry. Not only do the 'pirates' recall the traditions of Poole's privateering past: their role as Lords of Disorder, who are vanquished at the end of the day, serves to remind all users of the harbour of the need to treat one another in that 'civil loveing and courteous manner' that so impressed Richard Bramble.

Poole's thriving yacht clubs also played an important part in preserving the traditions of the harbour. By and large they enjoyed good relationships with the civic and port authorities. They had quickly re-established themselves after the

*(Above) At the end of the ceremony of Beating the Bounds, the 'Pirates' are sentenced by the Admiral to walk the plank.*
*(Below) Licensee's wife Mrs Nancy Broughton and barmaid Mrs June Waters were captured from the London Hotel by 'Pirates' and tied to a post in High Street.*

war years. As early as 1948 the Corporations of Poole and Bournemouth joined the Royal Motor, Poole, Poole Harbour, Parkstone and East Dorset Yacht Clubs to establish a 'Poole and Bournemouth Yachting Week.' In the early years, some of the races started at Bournemouth Pier, but when Bournemouth Corporation withdrew its support, the event was known as Poole Yachting Week, and all races were in the harbour and Poole Bay. It established itself as an annual festival for which scores of visiting helmsmen came to Poole to pit their skills against the locals, in vessels ranging from cruisers to Firefly dinghies.

It became the practice for the Mayor, Sheriff and Town Clerk of Poole to join the Commodore of Parkstone Yacht Club, and his wife, on board his motor yacht, to witness the start of racing. The local Press publicised the event with a photograph of the Commodore and his guests, who responded to the occasion by raising their glasses in salute. This was all good publicity: but no photographs were ever taken of an incident shortly after the start of the 1957 Week which was to carry its name to a much wider audience.

The Commodore and his party were coming alongside the club's jetty when his wife attempted to disembark before their launch had been securely moored. When she stepped out, she fell into the water, as the launch swung away behind her from the landing stage. In the scramble to rescue her, the Town Clerk ended up in the water with her, the Mayor, leaning over the side to help, became half-submerged, and was only saved by the Sheriff grimly hanging on to his leg! No Press photographer was on hand to record the occasion, as the waterlogged members of the official party hurriedly departed in search of a change of clothes. It was some time before news of the mishap leaked out and lurid accounts of it began to appear in newspapers around the world.

The annual passage race to Cherbourg, in which many leading citizens took part each Whitsun, was an important date in the calendar of the Poole cruiser fleet, and a precursor of the closer civic ties that were to develop between the two ports. These were given further encouragement by Herbert Ballam, the Mayor of Poole in 1963, who was himself a yachtsman and a competitor in the Cherbourg race.

Pressure on mooring space in the harbour was not at first so great that it needed close control by the Harbour Commissioners. Boat owners who did not wish to use the facilities of a yacht club were still free to lay their own moorings, having first obtained a licence from the Harbour Master and paid a modest annual fee related to the length of the hull. This system continued until 1960, when it was declared by Captain Horn to be unsatisfactory. The Commissioners decided that licence fees must be paid before moorings were laid and that all mooring buoys should show the licence number. In 1962, when it was reported that the number of licensed moorings in the harbour had doubled since 1957, to a total of 1,325, they set up a subcommittee to look at the problem again and proposed to double the licence fee.

By then the largely self-regulating and peaceful régime of the harbour was confronting a number of other threats from human intervention. The Commissioners had in 1960 felt it necessary to make byelaws requiring every vessel to navigate with care and caution, and to observe a speed limit of six knots in certain parts of the harbour. Fishermen were enjoined not to obstruct channels and fairways with their gear, and to cease the practice of drift-fishing in any fairway.

The Commissioners had for some time been concerned about the need to identify and register speedboats, whose activities were one of the major sources of annoyance to other users of the harbour, and sent their own launches out on regular patrols in an attempt to curb the problem. Ironically enough, one of the first persons to be fined the maximum of £5 by Poole magistrates under the Commissioners' new byelaws was a retired Lieutenant-Commander who was managing director of a leading Poole firm of boat dealers. He was alleged to have driven a high-speed motor boat at 25 to 30 knots past the Aunt Betty buoy, causing it to roll in a heavy wash. One man working on the buoy had to cling to it for safety, while another leaped into a launch.

The increasing popularity of yachting and boating in the affluent years around 1960 was reflected in the rapidly expanding membership of yacht clubs based in the harbour. Parkstone Yacht Club decided to restrict membership to owners and others with a genuine interest in sailing. For several years running, new records were set for the number of entries in Poole Yachting Week, which was organised from the club's premises. In 1962 the Royal Motor Yacht Club at Sandbanks played host to helmsmen of Olympic class yachts from fifteen nations. The regatta, organised by Poole Bay Olympic Sailing Association, helped to select those who would represent the United Kingdom in the 1964 Olympic Games at Tokyo. Poole Yacht Club, under the leadership of its Commodore, Robert Newton, who was Sheriff of Poole in 1950, had already announced a programme of vigorous expansion. It had outgrown its existing clubhouse at Hamworthy and planned to demolish it and build a larger one. There were also plans for a marina and 150 flats at Poole Harbour Yacht Club, Lilliput, for which the council refused permission, on grounds that they represented over-development of the site, and that an accommodation block 19 storeys high would be an intrusion into the harbour scene.

Private enterprise was eager to meet the increasing demand for yachting facilities. In 1961 an old established boatyard run for 35 years by Mr Walter Cobb and his brothers on the shores of Holes Bay at Hamworthy was taken over by a private company, Cobb's Quay Limited, which announced plans for dredging and reclamation to increase the number of berths to 300. During the same year, the borough council was faced with proposals to construct what it was claimed would be the largest yacht marina in Europe. It would provide berths adjacent to Poole Yacht Club at Hamworthy for about 1,500 vessels, averaging thirty feet in length, as well as a new yacht club, a 16-storey hotel and apartment block, and other facilities. The moorings would cover 38 acres of water, and a similar area would be reclaimed for the onshore developments.

Though West Sussex Marine Development Company later reduced its proposals to 750 moorings, and as early as 1960 had received the borough council's support in principle for a marina, it failed after 18 months of negotiation to secure planning permission, and exercised its right to appeal to the Minister of Housing and Local Government against the council's failure to determine its application. The company claimed it had 'bent over backwards' to meet objectors, who included Hamworthy residents, Dorset Wildfowlers, Southern Sea Fisheries District and a newly-formed company of oyster fishermen. The council, however, remained concerned about the effect on the harbour of any pollution from the marina basin.

It was hoped that a public inquiry into the scheme in August 1963 would decide that question once and for all. Dr James Hutton, Poole's Medical Officer of Health, said in his evidence that it would be extremely difficult to prevent the discharge of waste and sewage from yachts in the marina, and strict controls, including a right for the council to carry out inspections at any time, would be necessary. The inspector who held the inquiry sidestepped the issue, arguing in his report that it 'did not seem to be a matter which could be controlled under the Planning Acts.'

The inspector granted planning permission, subject to a number of detailed conditions. The company, which prior to the inquiry had hoped to start work in the autumn of 1963, and have the first section of the marina opened by the following April, had still not commenced work by October 1964, when it announced a further postponement.

Lack of progress on the scheme certainly came as a relief to those who were attempting to revive the once flourishing Poole oyster industry, which could trace its history back to Roman times. One project was launched by a group of scientists from Poole and District Technical Group. They began in about 1954 with a working capital of around £90. By 1959 hundreds of thousands of oysters had been laid in the harbour by the Poole Oyster Company, an Anglo-Dutch venture, which had a capital of £12,500. Another project in which the scientists were involved envisaged adding nutrients, such as phosphates and nitrates, to an enclosed area in the harbour, to improve the rate of growth of fish by increasing the concentration of marine algae on which they fed. It was also suggested that the loss of acidity caused by adding nutrients could be overcome by passing carbon dioxide gas, obtained from the flues of Poole Generating Station, through the water.

Another company, Oyster Fishermen (Poole) Limited, was formed by a group of twenty-five local fishermen. The first native Poole oysters to go to market for over a quarter of a century were lifted later in 1959. Bad weather for spratting in the autumn meant that oysters, and not sprats, were on the menu at the annual sprat supper given to local fishermen by members of Poole Harbour Yacht Club.

There were other signs of revival in the local fishing industry. The fleet of about 20 boats had been modernised and many had echo sounders for locating shoals. At one time, sprat fishermen relied on seagulls to lead them to a catch. Their electronic fish-finders showed that gulls often failed to detect huge shoals; and so the birds began following the boats. Inside the harbour, however, there had been complaints by fishermen that anything between two hundred and five hundred shags and cormorants were fishing there, and that each bird consumed up to sixteen pounds of fish a day. The Southern Sea Fisheries Committee agreed to reintroduce a bounty of 2s 6d a beak for birds shot by authorised marksmen.

Landings of plaice, skate, rayfish, sole and sprats at Poole in 1962 totalled 4,370cwt and were worth £9,099, while 922cwt of crabs, lobsters, winkles and other shellfish were also taken, worth £6,371. The total value of the catch, £15,470, was higher than those recorded at Weymouth or Wyke Regis. In 1963, Poole fishermen joined others from Channel ports in calls for the inshore fishing limit to be extended to twelve miles, after complaints that foreign trawlers had been seen in Poole Bay.

Following the formation of Poole and District Fishermen's Association, the annual fishing boat race, which it was feared might lapse through lack of public support, developed into a full-scale regatta, with races for rowing crews, and for dinghies and tenders powered by Poole-built British Seagull outboard motors. It became the custom for a Royal Navy fishery protection vessel to visit the port for the weekend of the regatta, and for crew members to take on the fishermen in pulling races and a Sunday morning football match.

Although thousands of Poole people were directly involved, in some way, with the various activities and events connected with their harbour, many times that number were fascinated, and almost bodily refreshed, just to be able to see its ever-changing vistas. In 1959 their long-held opinion was confirmed by its official designation as an area of outstanding natural beauty. In the same year John Betjeman, a frequent visitor, declared: 'Poole is a very beautiful place, and I don't think the official guide does it justice.'

Be that as it may, many visitors had sought the place out for themselves, and Poole people, though proud of their inheritance, had no wish to see the summertime congestion of their roads increased still further. During the busiest periods of the season, police were having to erect signs as far away as the New Forest to warn motorists: *'Sandbanks is already full!'*

*(Above) Poole Fishermen's Regatta.*
*(Below) Backwaters of Poole Harbour froze solid during the severe winter of 1962-63, and it was possible to walk across the ice to Long Island, where Mrs Joan Sydenham stayed on alone, trying to rescue seabirds from starvation.*

*Preparing for the start of the Seagull outboard motor race at Poole Fishermen's Regatta. Among the quayside characters are Reg Wills, Tom Davis, Fred Wills, John Buckby, George Buckby, Hubert Wills, Sid Hayes and Finn Tilsed.*

*'The Island is like any other private estate. If it wasn't surrounded by water, it would be surrounded by a wall'*

*John Bonham Christie, 1961.*

*Mrs Mary Bonham Christie in later years.*

# Brownsea Island Reborn

On 28th April 1961 a not unexpected event occurred which was bound to have serious implications for the conservation of Poole Harbour, and, indeed, its entire character and future destiny. Mrs Mary Florence Bonham Christie died at the age of 96 in a local nursing home, only a few hours after being taken ashore from Brownsea Island, which she had ruled in a solitary, frugal fashion for nearly 34 years.

It was as though, right up to the end of her life, this remarkable, strong-willed woman had been reluctant to forsake her secret, jealously guarded domain, in which she had decreed that living things were to be left to flourish undisturbed by human intervention.

In her day she was popularly regarded as a crank, a recluse, even as an object of fear. The black-clad Widow of Brownsea was not afraid of dealing with trespassers herself. She had also employed custodians who at times used force and intimidation to defend her shores, which by a quirk of law she owned right down to the low water mark. Boatmen who did not flinch amid storm and tempest were anxious about landing there, even when its 500 or so acres were guarded by no more than a handful of retainers.

While all around her the elegant achievements of previous owners were left to succumb to the forces of nature, Mrs Christie continued to reign against a background of muted antipathy and misunderstanding on the mainland. Partly this was due to her hostility to unwanted visitors: but it was also to do with the very location and recent history of the place upon which she chose to impose her simple and dogmatic notions of conservation.

Few wealthy women in their sixties, feeling the urge to live apart from the world, and close to nature, would have chosen the largest island in one of the world's largest natural harbours which, at the time Mrs Christie bought it, had a population of some 270 people, most of whom were forced to leave. Yet at the end of the day perhaps one should be more thankful for her unusual choice than critical of some of her other actions. She was, after all, merely the last in a long line of private owners who treated it as a personal kingdom in which they were free to live in whatever fashion suited them: and however controversial her ownership may have been, it lasted long enough to safeguard Brownsea from other forms of change until it could be permanently preserved as a properly managed nature reserve and a haven of peace and relaxation for all who care to come.

It was often said that under Mrs Christie, time stood still on the island, but that is only part of the story. Well before she bought it for a reputed £125,000 in 1927, it had become caught in a time-warp that extended back to its Edwardian heyday as a rich man's private paradise. Throughout her ownership there were Brownsea Islanders, born and bred, living on the mainland, who remembered only too well how different their lives had been before she arrived. William Dean, born on Brownsea in 1892, had been part of an establishment of ten gardeners, twenty servants, seven farm labourers, four handymen, two electricians, three painters, two bricklayers, one general labourer, and more than thirty other staff. Housing was free, and a man's average wage was eighteen shillings a week at a time when it was only fifteen shillings on the mainland. Entertainment for visitors, among them members of European royal families, included croquet, tennis, a nine-hole golf course, shooting, or walking through carefully tended avenues, gardens and woodland glades. Virtually all vestige of these would vanish, together with the farm, during Mrs Christie's stewardship.

At first, she was not so hostile to visitors. One August afternoon in 1929, she opened her island to them, at a charge of two shillings a head, in aid of the National Canine Defence League, in which she was said to have a deep interest. The tradition among the islanders was that she was so dismayed by what proved to be an unruly invasion that she vowed never to do so again, and all 'strangers' were prohibited from landing. She was widowed in 1931, when her husband and daughter died within a few months of each other.

Brownsea had seen the birth of the Boy Scout movement in 1907, when Baden-Powell held his first experimental camp there, under a Union Jack, riddled with bullet holes, that had been flown at the siege of Mafeking. Sadly, Mrs Christie's antipathy to visitors would also come to include Scout camps, and it was not until after her death, and with the support of her grandson John Bonham Christie, himself a former Scout, that the movement was able to re-establish any meaningful contact with its birthplace. Suggestions that a permanent memorial to Baden-Powell should be erected, or that in 1957, the first Scout camp should be re-enacted on Brownsea to mark the fiftieth anniversary of the movement, fell on deaf ears.

Not all would-be visitors, however, were as circumspect in their approach or intentions. The *Poole and Dorset Herald* reported in 1958 that Brownsea 'is a paradise of nudists who land there thinking they will be undisturbed. Young men and women sunbathe together on the beaches and dance naked in the grassy hollows.' Mrs Christie was not amused, even though her domain had been fulsomely described by a Wareham and Purbeck rural councillor as 'a garden of Eden,' following a public health inspection the previous year.

The official who carried out the inspection reported: 'In view of somewhat adverse press reports, and requests from various pests officers wishing to accompany me on the island's inspection, particular attention was paid to this subject. It can be authoritatively stated that such reports are unfounded, for during the inspection no evidence whatsoever was noted to indicate the presence of rats, mice, rabbits or any other vermin.

'Generally, it appears that the whole island is conducted in a fit and proper manner, and that housing and public health matters are in compliance with existing statutes.' He had no adverse comments to make and saw no reason for the council to take action. The chairman of the council declared that in view of rumours which had got around, it was a good job the matter had been cleared up.

It is possible to read between the lines of this report a rebuke to the rumour-mongers who murmured against the long term effects of Mrs Christie's autocracy, as well as a desire to re-state the principle that an Englishman's home, whatever form it takes, should be his castle, unless there are substantial breaches of one's obligations as a property owner. In the mid-twentieth century, the time was past when Brownsea could remain virtually exempt from the concerns of those on the mainland: but future generations will do Mrs Christie less than justice if they look for explanations beyond her simplistic approach to self-imposed responsibilities as landowner and conservationist. With hindsight it is possible to criticise her in both roles, yet remain fascinated by the single-mindedness with which she pursued them.

For someone with her fervent views about leaving nature to its own devices, the oil spillage which afflicted the island, a few months before her death, must have seemed like a devastating blow. In January 1961, the tanker *Esso Lyndhurst*, with a cargo of fuel oil destined for Poole generating station, was struck amidships in Brownsea Roads by the *Mogilev*, a Soviet cargo ship of 1,344 registered tons, whose bows were reinforced for navigation in ice-covered seas. About 60 tons of oil escaped into the water. Heavy pollution spread along the southern shores of Brownsea and Poole Harbour as far west as Newton Bay, Green Island and Furzey Island, and along the harbour shore at Sandbanks. At the end of the previous month there had been a spillage of approximately 6,000 gallons of oil into the harbour from an Admiralty establishment at Holton Heath. Minimum estimates by the Nature Conservancy in March 1961 were that, as a result of these two incidents, at least 300 birds of 32 different species were affected, of which 148 died, and that the toll would have been much higher if bird populations in the harbour had not been unusually low, due to mild weather.

*The formal gardens surrounding the Castle had become unkempt.*

Cleaning-up operations on Brownsea gave a number of unexpected visitors their first chance to see something of the island in the closing months of Mrs Christie's reign. There were by then only four people permanently living there: Mrs Christie, a boatman, and a middle-aged married couple. Mrs Christie lived alone in ground floor rooms in the vast Castle. She had a green parrot, named Joey, as a companion. Another 40 or so rooms, in the basement, and on three floors above her, were empty. Each morning at 9 o'clock, her post and breakfast were taken in to her. Sometimes she would already have been up for a couple of hours, feeding the peacocks. Still not stooped with age, she always rose early, washed in cold water, looked after herself throughout the day, until an evening meal was taken in, and never saw anyone without an appointment. She would rather strain her eyes to make use of the last moments of daylight than switch on an electric light. She expected her staff to light their homes with oil lamps whenever possible, because she thought it was cheaper than electricity. She wanted them to maintain a rigid time-table for visits to the mainland, which it was decreed should be infrequent, and only on certain specified days: but at her great age, it appeared she was being tolerated, rather than obeyed.

*Church Acre, before the National Trust set about the huge task of clearing overgrown areas to create open spaces and firebreaks.*

One visitor at this time, who came away almost overwhelmed by the atmosphere of decay that hung over the entangled acres and neglected buildings, wrote: 'When I saw the peacocks near the Castle again, there seemed to be something hateful and primitive in their strutting walk: as though rampant, disorderly Nature was being allowed to strip the bones of a civilisation, to triumph, with the shriek of a bird, over all that human wealth, skill and elegance had ever achieved.'

John Bonham Christie, who farmed at Marston, near Frome, inherited from his grandmother not only the ownership of Brownsea, but the daunting task of discovering a new role for this overgrown and largely run-down private estate. He therefore took steps to stimulate public interest in the problem of its future. In July 1961 a party of some 50 Scouts and Scouters made a pilgrimage to the site of Baden-Powell's camp. In October came the news that the island was up for sale. Mrs Christie had left £263,942, on which duty of £64,965 had already been paid; but no duty had so far been paid on the island, which she entailed to her grandson for life, expressing the wish that it should be preserved as a bird sanctuary. The dilemma was a simple one: after paying duty on the island there

*Churchyard, fields and farmyard had become trapped in a tangled web spun by Nature left to its own devices.*

would not be enough money left to do anything with it; and so it had to be sold. Tenders in excess of £200,000 were invited for the island, excluding the church and churchyard, which were not Mrs Christie's property, and the Villano, standing between the quayside and the Castle gardens, which would be retained as a holiday home by her grandson. Fifteen prospective buyers emerged, but only four tenders were finally submitted. Two were from private individuals, and below the reserve price, and two from developers whose schemes included luxury homes and a marina. It had already been estimated by one Sandbanks resident that, at current prices, Brownsea would be worth £1 million for housing development.

Such a prospect would nowadays be regarded by many people as little more than commercial vandalism, but in the early 1960s, at the start of a property boom fuelled by an obsession with high-rise buildings, it did not seem so out of place, and therefore had to be taken more seriously. So Wareham and Purbeck Rural Council, while opposing a planning application for 200 houses and a marina, declared its willingness to agree to a scheme at a much lower density, and to the development of a yacht marina in the area of the quayside.

Meanwhile, vandals of a less entrepreneurial vein had come to realise that without the legend of Mrs Christie to protect it, Brownsea offered a good place for some sport. In one episode, hundreds of panes of glass were smashed in unoccupied cottages. Graffiti were daubed on the walls. In another, the church was raided and coping stones thrown from the tower into the graveyard. The intruders carved their names on the lead roof. A painting of the Crucifixion in the family chapel, reputedly by Murillo, was holed and scratched. During his appearances as a prosecution witness at courts in Wareham and Swanage, John Bonham Christie agreed that a tremendous number of people had trespassed on the island during the summer.

Even counsel for the defence, at Dorset Quarter Sessions, found himself able to invoke the Brownsea *mystique* that was soon to pass into memory. 'For years,' he said, 'this mystery fairy island with a castle, impenetrable forests and strutting peacocks, has been a source of enticement to young dare-devils to show their courage by crossing Poole Harbour and taking some peacock feathers as souvenirs of their visit.' It was that, he suggested, and not a desire to commit sacrilege, that had lured his clients to the island.

In March 1962, more of Brownsea's treasures and curios were landed at Poole Quay. They included ancient cannon, antique marble ornaments, life size statues, stone urns and several other pieces that had once graced the lavish formal gardens around the Castle. Some were on their way to the Christie

*Some of Brownsea's treasures come ashore at Poole en route for salerooms and the Christie family home in Somerset.*

family home in Somerset, but others were to fetch a good price in salerooms. The Montagu Motor Museum at Beaulieu acquired a 1914 lorry brought ashore a few weeks earlier.

While prospective developers talked grandly of luxury homes and of the Castle possibly becoming the headquarters of the Royal Yacht Squadron, public demand for Brownsea to be saved continued to grow. In June 1962 it was announced that the island had been accepted in part payment of the duties on Mrs Christie's estate and had been given by the Treasury to the National Trust.

It was only the second time in its history that the National Trust had accepted a property without a financial endowment towards its upkeep, but within a matter of weeks, more than £70,000 of the £100,000 required had been pledged from a variety of charitable trusts and other sources. They included the John Lewis Partnership, which agreed to covenant £21,000 over seven years and to take a 99-year lease of the Castle and its grounds as a holiday centre for those working in its stores and factories. The National Trust saw this offer as relieving it of what it described as an expensive white elephant, for it regarded the Castle - rebuilt after a disastrous fire in 1896 - as having no historic interest or outstanding architectural merit. But some Poole councillors regarded the Partnership as having got too good a bargain. Be that as it may, the effect of the agreement was that the Castle and its activities would have virtually no direct part in the public enjoyment of Brownsea. The Partnership was certainly more successful than the previous incumbent in maintaining a low profile.

A public appeal was launched in Poole to raise the balance of £30,000 for the endowment fund. It reached this target in less than a year. The secretary of the appeal committee, Miss Helen Brotherton, was also secretary of the recently formed Dorset Naturalists' Trust. For the Naturalists' Trust, the campaign to save Brownsea came as a considerable challenge early in its existence, for it also involved accepting responsibility for the management of a nature reserve, including Saint Andrew's Bay, two lakes and a heronry, covering a substantial portion of the island. Leslie Miller, chairman of the appeal committee, declared that it was Miss Brotherton's enthusiasm, energy and singleness of purpose which enabled the project to go forward. Brownsea therefore holds a special place among the many achievements of what is now the Dorset Trust for Nature Conservation, of which she was later to become president.

A great deal of work had to be done before visitors could be admitted. Some derelict buildings would be eliminated, others converted to accommodation for wardens, staff, and the public. Fire breaks had to be cut in the woodlands and undergrowth, paths and open areas cleared. The considerable risk of fire and damage to wildlife meant it would be necessary to maintain resident staff on the island.

*The Bonham Christie family at the launching of their new motor cruiser from the Hamworthy yard of R A Newman and Sons.*

*A bouquet for Helen Brotherton as Leslie Miller, chairman of the appeal committee, pays tribute to her part in the campaign to save Brownsea.*

To help with the enormous task of clearing undergrowth, parties of boys from Portland Borstal Institution were sent to the island during September and October 1962. Seven young men, aged between 18 and 22, escaped while they were fishing on the quayside. They boarded John Bonham Christie's new motor yacht *Diligence of Marston*, which had been launched at R A Newman and Sons' Hamworthy yard only a few weeks earlier, and started it up. When it crashed into another motor yacht, causing nearly £1,400-worth of damage, they decided to make a run for it, taking cars and stealing food and clothes before they were caught. When the men appeared at Poole Quarter Sessions, the defence suggested the escapade had developed from something comparatively innocent. The Recorder, Malcolm McGougan, sentenced each of them to two years' imprisonment.

The official opening ceremony was performed by Olave, Lady Baden-Powell, on 15th May 1963. The widow of Scouting's founder had many local connections, having lived in Lilliput in the early years of the century, married in Saint Peter's Church, Parkstone, in 1912, and been made a Freeman of Poole in 1950. She was welcomed ashore by Alan Bromby, who was surely the ideal choice as the National Trust head warden. He had already worked on other

*(Above) On the 24th May 1942 the Luftwaffe had mounted a large raid on Poole but the Navy's 'Star Fish' site on Brownsea had deluded the Luftwaffe pilots to think that the island was Poole and it received 90% of the bombs intended for Poole and the cottages of Maryland were severely damaged and were later demolished.*

*(Left) Brownsea Islander Jack Battrick helps Olave, Lady Powell to plant a tree commemorating the island's rebirth as a National Trust property.*

*Arthur Primmer and Reg Giles, two members of the 1907 Scout camp on Brownsea, greet the Chief Guide.*

islands in Poole Harbour for the previous 15 years, and was a dedicated naturalist. At the end of her visit, she was taken to see the much overgrown site of the first Scout camp, where plans to provide new camping facilities for Scouts and Guides were already in hand.

It was an afternoon that recalled history, as well as making it. The mood was one of renewal, reunion and rejoicing; and in the ceremony of re-hallowing the church of St Mary, which was performed by the Archdeacon of Dorset, there were echoes of 'the Important and Very Interesting Proceedings' when the foundation stone was laid in July 1853. Guests felt a genuine sense of thanksgiving - as, no doubt, did Major Waugh, Brownsea's proud owner in 1853, when he declared: 'The good work has had a beginning - the end is in the hands of the Almighty.' But whereas Waugh was a private benefactor, whose munificence with borrowed money was to end in bankruptcy proceedings, those who gave thanks in 1963 did so not least because the island, and all that it meant, had been safely delivered into the keeping of a public custodian, and its future seemed finally assured.

*Church Acre in the spring of 1963 as the island prepared to open to the public. Alan Bromby, the National Trust head warden, surveys a job well done.*

On the morning of 16th May 1963 the island opened to the public for the first time. They were able to come by boat from Poole Quay, Shell Bay, Sandbanks and Rockley Sands. After paying a landing fee of two shillings and sixpence (12½p), or 1s 6d (7½p) for children, they were free to wander at will, except in the grounds of the Castle and the nature reserve. Private boats were allowed to land on the southern and western shores, where patrols of volunteer wardens collected the fees and kept an eye on visitors.

The unspoken fear in the minds of all those connected with the island was of an outbreak of fire. The volunteer wardens had already helped to protect it from such a danger while the National Trust prepared to take over: but Brownsea's immediate and enormous popularity with the public meant it was now receiving more visitors than ever before in its history - nearly 8,000 in the first fortnight alone. Emergency plans, which also involved Royal Marines from the amphibious training school at Hamworthy, had already been prepared by Dorset County Fire Brigade. On the afternoon of Sunday 2nd June 1963 those plans were put to the test. More than 80 acres of dense gorse and foliage

*The interior of Saint Mary's Church as it was in Mrs Christie's time.*

*The family chapel in Saint Mary's Church.*

were blackened as flames up to thirty feet high swept westwards along the southern shore. The blaze started at the viewpoint, a favourite spot with visitors, and raced downhill toward the site of the original Scout camp. Scouts working to clear a new camping ground joined firemen, Royal Marines, National Trust staff, and volunteer wardens in a three-hour battle to bring it under control. The strong north-east breeze was offshore at that point, which helped to prevent it spreading toward woodland at the centre of the island. A prevailing south-westerly wind might have resulted in a fire as devastating as that which swept the island in 1934 and took a week to quell. In July 1963 another fire broke out, again near the viewpoint on the southern shore; and once again an offshore breeze helped to confine it to ten acres. A 1922 bull-nose Morris Cowley touring car that had been on Brownsea since Mrs Christie arrived was pressed into service to help carry hoses to the scene.

Brownsea remained open until the end of September, when it closed to the public until April 1964. It had succeeded in surviving two of the gravest threats: the danger of fire and the sheer number of visitors. People from all walks of life, both serious naturalists and carefree holidaymakers, had taken the place to their hearts and rediscovered the unique character that endeared it to previous generations, the air of peace and tranquility which never seemed to forsake it, through all the unexpected twists of its sometimes turbulent history.

# Some of the People Involved

**ADAMS,** Geoffrey Pharaoh. Was taken prisoner by the Japanese in Singapore in 1941 while serving in the Army and employed on the building of the Burma-Siam Railway. Came to Poole from his native Midlands in 1955 and lived at Sandbanks with his wife Charmaine. Elected to Poole Borough Council in 1957 and soon made his mark as a councillor. A leading early advocate for the extension of Poole's shopping facilities.

**BARRON,** John Reynolds. The Borough Engineer of Poole from 1941 to 1963, he came to Poole in 1937 as deputy Borough Engineer after serving at Scunthorpe and Wembley. Until the appointment of Geoffrey Hopkinson (q.v.) he was also responsible for town planning control and architectural services. He was succeeded by Robert **HAWKER,** who had been Deputy Borough Engineer since 1951, after notable war service with the Royal Engineers at El Alamein and in Italy, for which he was awarded the DSO and OBE.

**BISGOOD,** Jeanne Mary. A barrister who was soon a leading member of the borough council after her election in 1955. Took over the chairmanship of Poole Committee for Education from Alderman Simmonds in 1958. A magistrate on the Poole Bench.

**BRAVERY,** Geoffrey. Councillor from 1940; Sheriff 1947-48, Alderman from 1952, when he was elected Mayor. Chairman and managing director of Capital and Counties Electric Theatres Limited, which had three cinemas in Poole, one in Bournemouth, and one in Wimborne. Vice-chairman of East Dorset Hospital Management Committee for 20 years. In 1963 he was made a member of Wessex Regional Hospital Board and a Governor of Saint Thomas's Hospital in London. The League of Friends of Poole Hospital was inaugurated during his mayoralty in 1952.

**BRIGHT,** Joseph. A baker who had earlier come from Wimborne and who twice became Britain's champion baker, with premises in High Street and a large bread delivery service until supermarkets cut prices and made deliveries uneconomic. He served on the council from 1930, was Sheriff in 1936, and was Mayor

*Joseph Bright.*

continuously from 1938 to 1945, during the whole of the war years. He was chairman of the Parks Committee from 1951, during the creation of Turlin Moor Recreation Ground and Rockley Sands holiday camp, and when speedway and greyhound racing were established at the Stadium. The Conservative caucus decided in 1961, when he was 78, that he was too old to be supported for election as Alderman for another six years. He therefore resigned and successfully put himself up for election as a councillor! He finally resigned from the council in 1964.

**BROTHERTON,** Helen. One of the founders of Dorset Trust for Nature Conservation. Established the Portland Bird Observatory in a disused lighthouse at Portland Bill, opened by Peter Scott in 1961. Earlier had been the active secretary, with Councillor Miller as chairman, and John Kay, deputy borough treasurer, as treasurer, of the public appeal for funds to endow Brownsea Island as a National Trust property and bird sanctuary.

**BUTLER,** Arthur Northcroft. Inherited Butler's Department Stores, with main premises in High Street and branches at Boscombe, Winton, Parkstone and Wimborne, and a brush factory in the old Poole Foundry building. Was officer commanding the Home Guard's 'Poole Redoubt' in World War II. Normally a shy, retiring man, he was a fervent opponent of the extension of Poole's shopping facilities into Longfleet. First elected to the borough council in 1946, he was Sheriff in 1957 and Mayor in 1958.

**CAROL,** Prince. In 1957 the Portuguese court accepted the claim of M. Mircea Lambrino, a Parisian bookbinder, to be the lawful son of the Crown Prince of Romania. The judgement was confirmed by the French courts and M. Lambrino became Prince Carol of Romania and entitled to a share of the Hohenzollern inheritance. It later transpired, however, that his inheritance was still in trust and that none of the capital could be spent by him on 'running expenses.'

**CARTER,** Herbert Spencer. Alderman of Poole 1904-48, Freeman 1928, Mayor on five occasions, and chairman of Poole Committee for

Education. He died in 1956 and the first secondary school to be built after the war was called after him.

**CASS,** Richard (Bob). Appointed Deputy Town Clerk of Poole in 1956. Previously with Plymouth City Council during redevelopment of the war-damaged city centre. Particularly active in administrative and legal work associated with the borough council's development proposals.

**COLE,** William Henry. The *enfant terrible* of Poole Borough Council at the time. A Poole man, born in Lagland Street, who claimed Sir William Phippard, three times mayor of Poole in the early 1700s, as an ancestor. With his brother inherited an undertaker's business in the Old Town and was passionately in favour of Poole becoming a county borough, but equally passionately against increased shopping facilities and the development of Ladies' Walking Field. Sheriff 1954, Mayor 1960.

**ELMES,** Frank. Retired in 1957 as Superintendent in charge of Poole police division, after serving for 30 years in Dorset Constabulary, and launched on a new career as writer, broadcaster and disc jockey. From 1959 introduced the BBC West Region request programme *Very Much at Home*, which ran for more than 400 editions.

**FERGUSON,** Alasdair. Poole industrialist and businessman. Born in Glasgow 1919, awarded DSC and bar, and mentioned in despatches, during service with the RNVR in World War II. Director of Hamworthy Engineering Limited from 1951, and chairman of a holding company owning Bourne Steel Limited and other local companies.

**GILLARD,** Frank. West of England controller of the BBC, of which he later became a Governor. Established an early unattended studio in the old Branksome Urban District Council offices. He also arranged many *Any Questions?* broadcasts from Poole, as well as producing a programme on its history and character.

**GOULD,** Donald Jack. Died in 1958, aged 46, after nine years as editor of the *Poole and Dorset Herald*, to which he brought a trenchant style of journalism that matched his 23-stone bulk and outspoken manner. Was also team manager of Poole Speedway until a disagreement with co-promoters Leonard Matchan and Geoffrey Bravery.

**GRIBBLE,** Bernard Finegan. Poole artist, specialising in maritime subjects, who had been an official Government naval artist during World War I. He gave many of his paintings to the town, plus eight coloured pictures of 1750 of Raphael's original designs of the Vatican, of which there had been only two copies. The Corporation loaned the pictures to Poole Technical College in 1955. He died in 1962, aged 89.

**HASKINS,** Wilfrid Thomas. Educated at Parkstone Grammar School, and later president of the Old Parkstonians. After training in horticulture at Wisley and in Holland and Germany, took over the Coy Pond Nurseries which his father has established in 1882, on the death of his brother John. Interested in youth clubs and sport. Founded Poole Athletic Club during his mayoralty in 1962. Chairman of the planning committee, 1957. Sheriff 1959. Alderman 1961, Mayor 1962. An 'independent Conservative' who, like a number of his colleagues, considered that politics had no place in local government.

**HAWKER,** Robert, See **BARRON**.

**HAYNES,** Alfred Beaumont. Pharmacist of Broadstone, brother of D A Haynes (q.v.). A member of the borough council from 1936 to 1967, he was Sheriff in 1940, and the first Broadstone member of the council to be Mayor in 1949. He was the energetic chairman of the Civil Defence Committee for the south-east of Dorset during the Cold War years, for which his efforts were rewarded with the MBE.

**HAYNES,** Donald Albert. A pharmacist of Parkstone and long-time chairman of Poole Health Committee. He joined the borough council in 1929, and was Sheriff in 1946 and Mayor in 1948. He was chairman of the committee established to provide shelter and help on Brownsea Island for the hundreds of Dutch and Belgians who had taken to boats to escape from the invading German Army in 1940. He was chairman of Poole Magistrates and of the local disablement advisory committee, which established workshops for the disabled in Alder Road. Mayor 1946. Died in 1962, aged 70.

**HESSION,** Rev. Brian. Former Vicar of Aylesbury, religious writer and broadcaster, who founded the Dawn Trust religious film organisation, through which he got to know such Hollywood stars as Mary Pickford and Charles Chaplin. Taken ill

*The Reverend Brian Hession.*

while visiting America in 1954 and given three days to live, but survived a major cancer operation. Became a national celebrity after the success of his book *Determined to Live* and founding Cancer Anonymous, which aimed to give others a chance to fight back against the fear, ignorance and secrecy surrounding the disease. Bought Greystoke, the former home of Lord Lyle, in Canford Cliffs, in

*Firemen tackle the blaze that destroyed the Reverend Brian Hession's Greystoke Hotel at Canford Cliffs.*

1954, and ran it as a hotel until a disastrous fire in 1960. Had no less than ten operations as well as cobalt treatment before he died in September 1961, just after publication of his last book *The Pinnacle of Faith*.

**HOPKINSON,** Geoffrey. Appointed Poole's first chief planning officer and Borough Architect in July 1960. Previously deputy chief architect to Bracknell New Town Development Corporation. He had earlier served with Northampton and Derby Councils. He became responsible for planning control and the positive planning and design of Poole's redevelopment.

**HUTTON,** James. A Scotsman. A doctor of medicine who succeeded Dr Chesney as Medical Officer of Health for Poole. Responsible for the public health of the borough, the school health service, and the port health service.

**INGHAM,** Arthur A. Borough Education Officer from 1959. A Yorkshireman who had the difficult task of running Poole's education service under the dual control of the borough and county councils.

**JULYAN,** H W H. 'Bill' Julyan was Borough Treasurer of Poole from 1941-58. Served in the 2nd Dorsets during the invasion of Gallipoli in World War I. Member and one-time chairman of Poole Rotary Club and treasurer of the Borough Scouting Association. He was succeeded by Bernard COX, his deputy, who had earlier served with Weymouth Corporation.

**KENYON,** Wilson. Solicitor and Town Clerk of Poole. A Yorkshireman, the first non-Poole man to hold the post, he was appointed in 1933 and died in office in 1956.

**LLEWELLIN,** John Jestyn. Born 1893, from 1945 first Baron Llewellin of Upton, PC, GBE, MC. Barrister, MP for Uxbridge 1929-45. He held a number of important Government appointments during World War II, including Minister for Aircraft Production and Minister of Food. Governor General of the Federation of Rhodesias and Nyasaland from 1953 until his death in Salisbury, Rhodesia, in 1957. His ashes were interred in Salisbury [now Harare] Cathedral.

**LLEWELLIN,** Margaret Mary. The first woman to hold the offices of Sheriff of Poole (1949) and Mayor of Poole (1951 and 1953). Resigned from the borough council in 1954 to act as hostess to her brother, Lord Llewellin, in Salisbury, Rhodesia.

**LLEWELLIN,** William Wigan, OBE. Elder brother of Lord Llewellin. Pioneer of the 'open' prison and Borstal system after 1922, when he took charge of Portland Borstal Institution. Following his retirement from the service in 1949 became a Dorset magistrate in 1950, and High Sheriff of Dorset in 1956. Gave Upton House and adjoining land to the Corporation and moved to Bere Regis, where he died in 1961, aged 72.

**LLOYD-ALLEN,** Arthur. An accountant who served with the War Department in Northern Ireland and later, with the Treasury in the Middle East. After the war established a practice in Parkstone. Elected to the borough council 1948, Alderman 1959, Sheriff in 1955, Mayor in 1957.

*Arthur and Peggy Lloyd-Allen, Mayor and Mayoress of Poole, 1957.*

As chairman of the borough council's finance and development committee from 1952, he became the leading advocate of the redevelopment of Poole. In 1954 he was elected a member of the general purposes committee of the Association of Municipal Corporations, and later became its vice-chairman. Member of the BBC West Regional advisory committee 1958-62.

**MATCHAN,** Leonard. Accountant and entrepreneur. A book-keeper with Max Factor, the Hollywood cosmetics maker, he became 'Lipstick Leonard' as its European manager. Became a Labour member of the borough council and stood as Parliamentary Labour candidate for Poole in the 1951 General Election. With his colleague Edward Webster he bought Cope, Allman, a small furniture manufacturer, for £800 in 1956, and turned it into a mini-conglomerate which by 1967 comprised 150 companies including steel, pharmaceuticals, one-armed bandits, packaging and transport. Being a socialist, he said, was 'a luxury millionaires can afford.' He left Poole in 1957 and bought the small Channel island of Brecqhou, from which he commuted by private plane to the mainland. He became honorary life president of Cope Allman International on his retirement in 1976, and died in 1987.

**McGOUGAN,** Malcolm. A practising barrister who was appointed Recorder of Poole in 1954 and continued in this office until Poole Quarter Sessions were abolished with the introduction of the Crown Court system. In his early years he favoured probation, rather than custodial sentences, but in 1958, when past offenders began to reappear in his court, and the number of local crimes during the quarter had increased by 126 to 462, he announced: *'I have been too lenient. Sterner methods will have to be adopted.'*

**PAPA,** Benedetto. A familiar figure on the streets of Poole, during more than half a century as a wandering musician in the south and west of England. In 1962, at the age of 73, he left Mr Angelo Zollo's lodging house in West Street, Poole, where he had lived for some ten years, and retired to his native Italy to live with his family near Monte Cassino.

*Benedetto Papa, served in the Forces in World War I. Afterwards he travelled with his barrel organ and monkey and was a favourite sight in Poole in the 'fifties.*

*John B Score, one of the pioneers of the nuclear disarmament campaign in Poole, regularly refused to pay the proportion of his rate demand attributable to Civil Defence expenditure.*

**PILKINGTON,** Captain Sir Richard Anthony, KBE, MC. Born 1908 in Lancashire. Son of managing director of Pilkington Glass Company of Saint Helens. A Captain in the Coldstream Guards, he was among the last to leave Dunkirk and was awarded the MC. MP for Widnes 1935-50. Civil Lord of the Admiralty 1942. MP for Poole 1951-64. Lived at Ferry House, Sandbanks, with wife and three daughters. Awarded KBE 1961.

Election results:

| | |
|---|---|
| 1951 R A Pilkington (Con.) | 26,998 |
| L J Matchan (Lab.) | 18,346 |
| W Ridgway (Lib.) | 5,029 |
| 1955 R A Pilkington (Con.) | 26,594 |
| F C Reeves (Lab.) | 17,032 |
| J C Holland (Lib.) | 5,750 |
| 1959 R A Pilkington (Con.) | 26,956 |
| A Williams (Lab.) | 15,325 |
| J C Holland (Lib.) | 8,735 |

**REEVES**, Frederick Charles, OBE, MM. Native of Winchester, whose family moved to Upper Parkstone, where his father ran the local Scout troop. Served in the Army in World War I and was awarded the Military Medal. He later suffered a gas attack and was taken prisoner. Elected to Poole Borough Council in 1931, and the leading advocate for constructing the Municipal Buildings. Deputy Controller of Civil Defence in World War II. He was a strong leader of the Labour caucus on the council, and agent to Poole Labour Party. Sheriff in 1937, Poole's first Labour Mayor in 1954, and Parliamentary candidate in the 1955 general election. He died in 1959.

**ROWE,** Frederick George. Served in World War II with the Ministry of Works on the construction of airfields in the Near East. Founded his own building firm after the war. Elected in 1959 to the borough council, he soon made his mark, becoming chairman of the Parks Committee on the resignation of Alderman Bright in 1961.

**SCORE,** John B. Former R.A.F. officer who became a pioneering campaigner for nuclear disarmanent. He picketed the Labour Leader Hugh Gaitskell during a visit to Poole, urging him to honour party conference decisions on the issue. He was also an active member of local ratepayers' associations. His other interests included witchcraft and flying saucers.

**SHERRIN,** Thomas William. Elected to the borough council in 1952, Sheriff in 1961 and Mayor in 1964. A big, burly man who had a distinguished record of war service as a naval officer, he weighed almost 25 stones in full mayoral regalia, and his stentorian voice was a feature of meetings of the council. He had a particular interest in swimming, having been captain of both Hampshire and Dorset water polo teams. The leading advocate for Poole to have its own swimming baths. He was awarded the MBE for services to the Sea Cadet Corps.

*Guy Sydenham.*

**SYDENHAM,** Guy. Head thrower at Poole Pottery, where he began work as soon as he left school. His personality and skills were familiar to countless visitors to the Pottery, and a major factor in its success in the post-war period. Later he established his own pottery on Long Island, making salt-glazed stoneware entirely from materials found there.

**VALENTINE,** John Albert ('Jack'). Came to Poole in the Thirties after retiring from the Navy and found it was a place he could never leave. Founded the Open Store in High Street with a capital of £5 and became a highly knowledgeable antique dealer and collector. As President of the Society of Poole Men for six years from 1959 he championed the cause of conservation in the Old Town, where

*Jack Valentine*

he lived at West End House, West Street.

**WELLS,** Charles William. Councillor from 1945, Sheriff in 1953, died suddenly in 1957, at the age of 63, only ten days before the end of his term of office as Mayor. Born in Bournemouth, he became a passionate 'Poole-ite' and was a lifelong supporter of the trade union, Labour and Co-Operative movements. He was funeral service director of Parkstone and Bournemouth Co-Operative Society.

**WHEATLEY,** Sir Mervyn James, KBE, DL. Born in Poole in 1880, joined the Dorset Regiment in 1900, fought in the South African war 1900-02, and was among the members of Dorset Volunteer Active Service Company who were made Freemen of Poole in 1901. After 20 years in the Sudan political service he returned to Poole and became Mayor in 1936, commander of Poole Home Guard, 1940-45, MP for East Dorset and Poole 1945-51, and was appointed a Government Whip by Churchill in 1948. A former borough and county alderman, he became a deputy lieutenant of Dorset and received a knighthood in 1952, and was chairman of Poole Conservative Association for 14 years from 1953.

General Election results:
1945: East Dorset

| | |
|---|---|
| Lt.-Col. M J Wheatley (Con.) | 26,561 |
| Lt-Cmdr. C Fletcher-Cooke (Lab.) | 25,093 |
| Lt.-Col. J A H Mander (Lib.) | 8,975 |

General Election 1950: Poole

| | |
|---|---|
| Lt.-Col Mervyn J Wheatley (Con.) | 24,344 |
| Lt.-Col Evelyn M King (Lab.) | 17,831 |
| William Ridgway (Lib.) | 6,531 |

**WOOLLARD,** Commander Claude Lombard Aubrey. Born in Richmond, Surrey, in 1882, claimed to have travelled more than three million miles by land and sea. On the barque *Penrhyn Castle* during a total of 1,093 days at sea, he made three voyages around the world and rounded Cape Horn on five occasions. He was the owner of an 1895 Leon Bollee tricar reputed to be the oldest car still running on public roads. He founded the Girls' Nautical Training Corps, which was based in Poole Harbour on board the sailing vessel *English Rose.* A Freeman of both Paris and Honfleur, he was a prominent member of local Anglo-French societies.

*Commander Claude Woollard.*

## SPORTING

**ALLISS,** Peter. The professional at Parkstone Golf Course 1957-70. In the first year of his appointment won the Spanish, Portuguese and Italian Open championships. Won the British PGA championship in 1957, 1962 and 1966, played in eight Ryder Cup matches between 1953 and 1969, and won many European Open championships.

**BAKER,** Percy. A Poole Park bowler who won the British Open bowls championship in 1932, 1946, 1952 and 1960, and the silver medal in the Empire Games of 1955, and helped the club to win ten national bowls championships in the decade.

**BISGOOD,** Jeanne. One of the leading golfers of the 1950s when she won the English Ladies' championship three times in seven years. She played in the Curtis Cup team in 1950, 1952 and 1954, and later in 1970 was the non-playing captain.

**GARRETT,** Maureen (née Ruttle). A member of the English Curtis Cup team in 1948 and a member of the governing body of the Ladies' Golf Union for many years.

**JONES,** Courtney. World Ice Dancing champion 1957-1960, first with June Markham (1957-58) and then with Doreen Denny. Jones and Denny retired in 1961, having been unable to defend their world title that year, because the championships were cancelled after the deaths of 17 American skaters in an air crash.

**RHODES,** Wilfred. Cricketing genius who in 1953 came to live in Poole with his daughter, Mrs Burnley, and later became a vice-president of Poole Sports Council. Born 1877, he made his debut for his native Yorkshire in 1898. During 32 years in first-class cricket he scored 39,797 runs, took 4,187 wickets, and 16 times achieved the feat of scoring 1,000 runs and taking 100 wickets in a single season. Fred Rowe (q.v.) took a leading part in arranging a dinner at the Branksome Tower Hotel in honour of the 80th birthday of the most famous living cricketer of the time. Mr Rhodes had become blind before moving to Poole, where he later died in Belmont Court Home for the Blind, Parkstone.

**UBER,** Betty. One of the best doubles players in the annals of badminton, who represented England for 25 years. On her retirement in 1956 the cup presented to the winners of the Women's World Team badminton championship was named after her, and the Uber Cup is still played for.

**WHITCOMBE,** Reg. Golf professional at Parkstone, who won the Open golf championship in 1938. He died in 1957 and was succeeded by Peter Alliss (q.v.).

# Index

# Picture Index